ONE WEEK AFTER EASTER 2024 is MERCY SUNDAY IN ... CHURCH : MO.

DEAR ADAM,

YOU ARE CREATED BY GOD IN GOD'S LIKENESS.

ONLY JEWS, AND CHRISTIANS, AND MESSIANIC JEWS TODAY BELIEVE IN THIS. DIGNITY OF HUMAN PERSON.

ALL OTHER RELIGIONS "REBIRTH" RELIGIONS TAKE OUT THE DIGNITY OF HUMANS BY REDUCING HUMANS TO INSECTS OR RATS. (HINDUISM). BUDHA SAID, THAT HE IS NOT A GOD AND ALSO REJECTED 3 MILLIONS HINDU GODS, BUT BEING HIMSELF A HINDU HE "LEFT" "REBIRTH" MIS- TAKE FOR HIS FOLLOWERS.

LUCKILY, MOST OF JEWS (IN OLD TESTAMENT OF BIBLE) ARE CIRCUMSCISED AND BELIEVE IN 10 COMMANDEMENTS FROM GOD: ABRAHAM, MOSES, KING DAVID AND ... JESUS!

WOMEN DID NOT NEED TO READ OLD TESTAMENT, ESPECIALLY TILL AGE 40 (TIME TO RAISE KIDS), FROM TIME OF JESUS & AFTER RESURECTION AND ASCENSSION — ALL WOMEN ARE ALLOWED TO READ THE BIBLE, BUT CAN NOT BE PRIESTS (IN CATHOLIC CHURCH).

IN GENESIS 3:15 (PROTOEVANGELIA) GOD PROMIS- SED TO SEND ANOTHER WOMAN THAN ADAM'S WIFE (EVE), IF YOU MY GRANDSON READ THIS SENTENCE, YOU CAN SEE GOD'S PLAN. IN PRE-HISTO- RIC TIME, FOR WOMAN "FULL OF GRACE, WHO WILL BE MOTHER OF MESSIAH, LIKE is SAID, IN NEW TESTA- MENT — LUKE 1:26-56 ANNUNCIATION).

ALSO JESUS SAID: "BEFORE MOSES, I AM" — SO OUR CHRISTIAN GOD IS: GOD FATHER, SON & HOLY SPIRIT = HOLY TRINITY. NOTICE THAT "SINGLE GOD OF JEWS" — IS ... PLURAL! "LET'S CREATE HUMAN IN OUR LIKENESS" ♡ G-ma Martha

What These Girls Knew

What These Girls Knew

How Girls Back Then Talk to Us Today

THELMA WELLS

Published by

THOMAS NELSON

Since 1798

www.thomasnelson.com

We'd love to hear from you about your experience with this book. Please go to **www.thomasnelson.com/letusknow** for a quick and easy way to give us your feedback.

Love to read? Get excerpts from new books sent to you by email. Join Shelf Life, Thomas Nelson's FREE online book club. Go to **www.thomasnelson.com/shelflife**.

WHAT THESE GIRLS KNEW.

Published in Nashville, Tennessee, by Thomas Nelson, Inc.

Unless otherwise indicated, Scripture quotations used in this book are from the Holy Bible, New International Version (NIV). Copyright © 1973, 1978, 1984, International Bible Society. Used by permission of Zondervan Bible Publishers.

Other Scripture passages are from these sources: The King James Version (KJV) of the Bible. *The Message* (MSG), copyright © 1993. Used by permission of NavPress Publishing Group. The New American Standard Bible® (NASB). Copyright © 1960, 1962, 1963, 1968, 1971, 1972, 1973, 1975, 1977, 1995 by The Lockman Foundation. Used by permission. The New King James Version (NKJV), copyright © 1982, Thomas Nelson Publishers, Inc. Used by permission. The Living Bible (TLB), copyright © 1971 by Tyndale House Publishers, Wheaton, Ill. Used by permission. The Holy Bible, New Living Translation (NLT), copyright © 1996 by Tyndale Charitable Trust. Used by permission of Tyndale House Publishers, Wheaton, IL.

Library of Congress Cataloging-in-Publication Data

Wells, Thelma, 1941–
     What these girls knew : how girls back then talk to us today / Thelma Wells.
       p. cm.
     ISBN-10: 0-8499-0175-8 (hardcover : alk. paper)
     ISBN-13: 978-0-8499-0175-1 (hardcover : alk. paper)
     1. Women in the Bible. 2. Christian women—Religious life. I. Title.
BS575.W45 2007
220.9'2082—dc22   2006036948

Printed in the United States of America

07 08 09 10 01 QW 9 8 7 6 5 4 3 2

There are thousands, maybe millions, of women all over the world who need to know the ins and outs of BEEing the best person they can bee. The words and actions of the biblical women featured in this book speak to us to educate us, encourage us, and inspire us to strive toward a better life.

I dedicate this book to those who will read these words and search for the messages, then link them to their souls and embrace them with their lives. Like these women of long ago, I hope you too will inspire others for years to come.

Some of our men ran out to see, and sure enough, Jesus' body was gone, just as the women had said.

—Luke 24:24 TLB

Contents

Acknowledgments

FOR MORE THAN A DECADE, THOMAS NELSON Publishers has been publishing my work under the W Publishing Group imprint. I appreciate the opportunity to publish for one of the largest Bible publishers in the world. And what a privilege now to write about some of the women in the Bible who speak to the world, but specifically to the Women of Faith audiences throughout American and Canada. The editors at W Publishing saw the need for these women to be addressed by other women, women of generations long ago, and allow them to speak to us today. The W Publishing editors suggested this project, and I'm delighted they did so.

Thanks to Mary Graham, Carolyn Denny, Amy Chandy, and all the godly women in these organizations who had the insight and foresight to help shape this book. I hope it will help us all learn from these biblical women in a way we might not have thought of before. As we study their lives and their lessons, we can see similarities to our own lives today.

Thanks also to Sue Ann Jones, a dedicated editor who worked diligently with me in one of the most testing times of my life. Thank you! I appreciate you!

❦ 1 ❧

Stepping Up, Standing Still, or Running Away, God Uses Us

The wind blows where it wishes, and you hear the sound of it, but cannot tell where it comes from and where it goes. So is everyone who is born of the Spirit.

—John 3:8 NKJV

WAY OUT IN WEST TEXAS, A COUPLE HUNDRED miles from my home in Dallas, there's an amazing sight as you drive down the interstate. Along the edges of the mesas there are dozens, maybe hundreds, of huge wind turbines. These giant towers (usually 164 feet tall, according to a state Web site) are used to convert wind into electrical energy. And out there in West Texas, the wind is *always* blowing.

The line of turbines seems to roll along the jagged edges of the mesas for miles, and all along the way, you can see the turbines' long fan blades slowly turning in the breeze, a modern adaptation of the old-fashioned windmill. But every so often there's a turbine that's stopped, and when you see it, you can't help but wonder why.

Why would one turbine be stopped when the turbines on either side of it are whirling away? The same wind that makes those other blades slice through the air must also be available to the turbine that's stopped. But something—or someone—has interfered. Maybe something in the turbine's mechanism has broken. Or maybe someone somewhere has thrown a switch that locks the blades into place so they can't respond to the wind.

I'm no engineer, but I can't help but think that, if the wind blew hard enough, it could break the lock that has shut down the turbine, and those blades *would* turn. Or maybe the resistant turbine would be blown over by a hard wind, striking other towers as it falls and toppling them too.

Thinking about those machines and how they respond to the wind—or don't—I'm reminded of how we as Christians respond—or don't—to the power of the Holy Spirit blowing through our lives. When we allow ourselves to be empowered by God's will, we're able to generate goodness and accomplish work we could never dream of doing on our own. But sometimes we're resistant; sometimes we don't respond to his presence, to the rush of his Word breathed into our spirit. Then, it seems to me, one of two things happens: Either God uses us anyway, overcoming our locked attitudes to do his work, one way or another—and maybe in a "way" we'd hoped wouldn't happen. Or, when we're locked in stubbornness, the consequences of our resistance may be that we take a fall.

The point is, God *will* fulfill his plan for us. He *will* use us to achieve his purpose, whether or not we willingly cooperate with him. As the saying goes, We can't *all* learn by example. Some of us have to *be* the example others learn from!

This book is about some of my favorite women of the Bible whose behavior and stories have generated lessons that have impacted my life. God has used these women—with or without their cooperation! For the most part, they were common folks. Some of them were wealthy; others were poor. Some were famous; some were barely known. But whether they did great things or a single small gesture, somehow they made an impact that has lasted thousands of years. Once again I think of those wind turbines and imagine how their power is being used. Maybe it just illuminates a single porch light burning to welcome home a returning loved one. Or maybe it powers the NASA computers in Houston that guide the space shuttle back to earth.

The power of these women's stories can have an impact just as varied. I love to read them again and again, always discerning something enlightening about how God uses them to speak to us all these thousands of years later.

And by the way, this book isn't just about my favorite Bible heroines. It's also about some other famous—or maybe I should say *infamous*—women of the Bible. They certainly can't be called my favorites; the truth is, a couple of 'em were more like floozies! But I've been impacted by their stories as well. Their lives tell us about what happens when we're resistant to God's will and get locked into hardhearted stubbornness that robs us of our potential to generate goodness. As you'll see, some of these women were downright mean; their hearts didn't respond at all to God's love and guidance. They were like the turbines that stand motionless and useless on the edge of the mesas . . . until that wind, which *could* have been a positive force for them, instead blows them over.

These wicked women caused harm wherever they went,

bringing down others as they fell into evil themselves. No Christian woman today wants to follow their lead; but we can certainly learn from what their stories tell us.

And here's one final thought: one way or another, the biblical women I'm talking about in this book know *today* that Jehovah God is the all-powerful, omnipotent Creator. If they didn't know that fact all those thousands of years ago when he was trying to guide their steps and lead them in the pathways of righteousness, well, sister, you can bet they know it now, wherever they are spending eternity!

It's like my husband, George, says about car headlights that are left on when the driver gets out of the car. One way or the other, those headlights *will* go off. The easy way is if the driver realizes the mistake and returns to turn them off, or if the car does what its maker designed it to do and turns off the lights automatically. The hard way is if the driver ignores the reminder that dings or if the car doesn't perform as it should. Then the burning headlights run down the battery until the whole car is as dead as a doorknob. Yes sirree, eventually those lights *will* go off!

Similarly, one way or another, the women I'm writing about here *do* know today that God is the supreme Ruler of the universe. Maybe, as believers, they knew it even before their stories were recorded for us to read centuries later. Maybe they learned it the hard way—as they stepped into eternity.

With a few exceptions, these gals would have been forgotten long ago except for something that happened to them. In most cases, they found themselves in situations they hadn't chosen—probably *wouldn't* have chosen if it had been left up to them. And they faced those dark or challenging situations in ways that set them apart. As a result, their stories have lived on through the ages to teach and inspire us thousands of years later.

Which brings us back to those West Texas wind turbines. When they respond to the wind and are used by it, they generate power that can do a lot of good for people who may live hundreds of miles away. I want to be like one of those towers, responding to God's will in a way that brings goodness to others. I already know what God can do. But I can always learn more, and I especially want to learn from these women who lived back in Bible times. Their stories speak to me, and I hope they'll speak to you also as we look at what they knew—and what we can learn from them.

❧ 2 ❧

Knowing What She Knew

If I just touch his clothes, I will be healed.

—Mark 5:28

WE DON'T KNOW HER NAME. NO ONE SEEMS TO have thought to ask it. She was just another face in the crowd, and I suspect that's the way she wanted it. She wasn't well, didn't feel good at all. The fact was, she'd had health problems—*female* problems—for twelve years. Those of us who've suffered our own female problems can understand why she probably preferred to remain anonymous. Can you spell *h-o-r-m-o-n-a-l?*

She'd been to many doctors, but none had been able to stop the flow of blood. Surely any woman of any era could understand how frustrated she must have been, how miserable she must have felt. Enduring such problems in today's disposable-everything, wash-and-wear world would be hassle enough. But imagine having such a problem for twelve years when nothing was reusable and laundry was scrubbed by hand on the riverbank.

So there she was in the crowd surrounding Jesus as he made his way through the streets. Apparently she wasn't strong enough or bold enough to push her way to the front of the mob to catch his eye. Matthew, Mark, and Luke all say, as they tell her story in their Gospels, that she "came up behind him."

We don't know who she was, but we can empathize with her anxiety that day, and we sure can't forget the lesson she taught us. It's one that's been told and retold millions of times for two thousand years, and it still astounds us today. The fact was, she'd been sick for twelve years, she'd seen many doctors who couldn't help her, and yet on that day she had such unshakable faith that she thought, "If I just touch his clothes, I will be healed" (Mark 5:28).

Matthew's account (9:20) says she touched "the edge of his cloak." The King James Version describes it as "the hem of his garment."

The hem? I wonder. *The edge of his cloak?* My mind tries to picture how *that* could have been the part of Jesus's garment she managed to touch amid the surging crowd. Could she have been knocked down by the mob as it moved by? And still she didn't give up? Her faith and determination were that strong?

Absolutely. And Jesus knew it. As soon as her fingertips brushed over the fibers of his garment, "he turned around in the crowd and asked, 'Who touched my clothes?'" (Mark 5:30).

Now, here's the funny part, if anything in this story can be seen as funny. Jesus was in the middle of a mob, with no telling how many people pressing up against him like he was some kind of rock star. (Actually, I guess you could say he was *The* Rock star of all times, right?) Anyway, he's got a mess of people clamoring around him, and suddenly he stops and asks who touched him.

The disciples, who are probably being battered and bruised trying to do security duty, are incredulous. "Who *touched* you, Jesus? Are you nuts?" they ask. "Can you see this crowd of crazy people here trying to trample us to tidbits so they can look you in the eye? We're all smashed in here together like grapes in a winepress, and you're asking who *touched* you? They've *all* touched you, Lord!" (I may have put just a tiny bit of personal interpretation on this passage; you can read the original in Mark 5:31.)

But Jesus wasn't kidding. He had felt power go out of him when the woman made her move, and now he was looking through the sea of faces to find her. Mark 5:33–34 tells the rest of the story: the woman, "knowing what had happened to her, came and fell at his feet and, trembling with fear, told him the whole truth."

Of course she wasn't telling Jesus anything he didn't already know. In fact, at that point they *both* knew what had happened. Jesus spoke to her to let the crowd in on the secret. He said, "Daughter your faith has healed you. Go in peace and be freed from your suffering."

Unfailing Faith

Oh, for the determined, undistracted, healing faith of that anonymous woman! Until Jesus spoke to her, she was a silent nobody in the crowd that day. But two thousand years later, the story of what she knew still speaks to us in an unforgettable way. She knew Jesus had the power to change her life for good. And I, for one, know he still has that power today.

I also know about "female problems." Back in 2005, as the Women of Faith tour headed into the busiest part of its season, I was getting very, very tired. But we were traveling so much, and I had so much going on, I thought getting tired was perfectly normal. There were other symptoms—"female" things—but not enough to alarm me, at least at first. But eventually the problems bothered me so much I went to the doctor's office for some tests, and when the reports came back he recommended a hysterectomy.

I talked to several women who'd had hysterectomies, and they said, "Oh, girl! That's gonna be the best thing for you. You'll be so happy. You'll feel so great after it's over!"

Let me just say, if you are one of those women who said those things to me, don't you be talking sweet to me now, OK? No, ma'am! If you do, I may give in to an overwhelming urge to hit you upside the head! Well, no. I wouldn't resort to violence, but I would certainly have some un-Thelma-like thoughts about you.

I agreed to have the surgery, and I laid out the schedule the doctor and I would follow. My last speaking engagement of the year was booked for December 7, and I would have the surgery December 8 and come home by December 11. A week later I would trot into the doctor's office for the follow-up exam, and by Christmas I would be presiding over my family's annual holiday celebration, as usual. A couple of weeks after that I would be in Florida, teaching a weeklong course for Master's International Divinity School. Shortly after that, the 2006 Women of Faith schedule would resume, and I would happily be back to normal (or as normal as I ever was) and on my way through a productive and rewarding year without any of the health problems that had necessitated the surgery.

That was my plan.

Once I announced to my doctor and the world in general what I would do, the prayer chains were activated, and I personally and fervently prayed that God would give me strength and courage to face this little procedure. Then I confidently headed off to the hospital on December 8, so happy I didn't know what to do. I told my friends and family, "I'm going to have a hysterectomy! I'm not worried about nuthin'! This is gonna be great."

Looking back several months later, I identify even more strongly now with the woman who reached out to Jesus that day so long ago. She had endured female problems for years longer than I'd had to deal with them, so she had suffered much more than I had. But we believed the same thing, and we were confident in what we knew: *Jesus could heal us*. So we both headed out the door of our homes with hope in our hearts and conviction in our faith.

Girl, I came through that surgery without a hitch and woke up that afternoon feelin' fine and feisty—well, except for that big incision stapled shut across my tummy. It slowed me down a little, but otherwise, I was my regular sweet, docile, and undemanding self. I said, "I want FOOD! Give me something to eat!"

And here they came with Jell-o, apple juice, and something they called broth. Well, that made me a little cranky. I said, "Y'all, this ain't food! I need more than this. I'm hungry!"

They said, "You can have all the broth you want."

Somehow I survived the all-liquid diet and set my mind on recovering, but as the hours passed, I sensed that something was wrong—so much so that when the doctor said I could be discharged on December 11, I told the hospital staff that, even though I *wanted* to go home, I didn't think I was ready.

"Oh, you just need to get home and get rested," the nurse told me. "Surgery takes a lot out of you—in more ways than one! You don't have a fever, and your body functions are normal, so you're definitely ready to go. And, anyway, you can get more diseases in the hospital than almost anywhere else. You're much better off at home than you are here."

I recognized that what she said was true, so off I went, ready to get well and live out the happy ending I knew would conclude this little surgical story. I still had some doubts about how quickly I would recover, because I was still having quite a bit of pain. But I trusted my doctor, and I trusted God, and I knew that, between the two of them, my healing *would* happen. After all, that was my plan.

LIVING OUT WHAT WE KNOW

I'm just imagining things here, but I believe the woman who reached out to Jesus also had a plan when she left her home that day. Maybe she pictured herself walking up and sitting down beside him in some peaceful setting, maybe while he was taking a lunch break. Maybe she planned to quietly and discretely explain her embarrassing request. Maybe she thought that, to bring about this miracle, he would place his hands on her head and pray for her. We can't know what she planned. We can only know what she *knew*.

She knew he could heal her. And knowing that, she may have had plans for what she would do when her health was restored. Maybe she planned to stop by a girl-friend's house on the way home and share the good news after her encounter with the Lord. Or maybe, like me, she was planning to host a big family event in a few days, and she looked forward to doing so without the pain, exhaustion, and general distractions she'd endured for such a long time. Or maybe not. Mark tells us the woman had "spent all she had" trying to find a cure for her problem. It's possible the woman was both desperate and destitute.

Either way, I picture her heading out confidently, knowing her life was about to change for the better. I imagine her hurrying down the road or through the streets, following her plan to find Jesus and speak to him.

Maybe a distant roar of voices or a billowing cloud of dust was her first indication that there was a hitch in her plan. Maybe she hadn't counted on a cacophonous crowd . . .

She may not have known that, when she saw him, Jesus would be surrounded by "a large crowd," as he made his way to heal someone else and she would have to fall back to Plan B. It turns out that an important person named Jairus, "one of the synagogue rulers," had asked Jesus to come place his hands on Jairus's daughter, who was dying (in Mark's account) or already dead (in Matthew's).

There's nothing in Mark 5 or Matthew 9 that indicates the woman in our story was also an important person in that area. To this day, we don't know who she was. As I said, we only know what she knew, and that's what is *really* important to us now.

If she had first thought she could talk to Jesus quietly about her problems, that plan changed drastically as she was caught up in the swirling crowd. We don't know how long she spent fighting her way forward through all the people, trying to get to him. We don't know whether, just as she reached him, she was knocked down. But whatever happened, she didn't give up. Maybe she wanted to tap Jesus on the shoulder, but just as she finally came up behind him, someone's foot tripped her or someone's arm hit her. So instead of touching him, she touched his cloak—and the bottom of his cloak, at that.

But her unfaltering faith made that enough. She was immediately healed.

WHEN OUR PLANS GET KNOCKED DOWN

I came home from the hospital, and sometime in the middle of the next week, I had a bad coughing spell. Usually if I had to cough or sneeze, I would hold a cushion over my tummy to keep from straining the surgical incision. But that coughing fit hit me when the cushion was nowhere near. I coughed and coughed and coughed without that familiar "shock absorber," and afterward I felt like little fish were swimming around in my stomach. Thinking now about the woman in the story, I liken my coughing spell to her seeing the dust cloud off in the distance or hearing the crowd clamoring for Jesus's attention. For both of us, it might have been the first inkling that things weren't going to be as easy as we'd hoped they would be.

I called the doctor's office, and the nurse asked me several questions then assured me everything sounded normal. But when I went back for the follow-up exam later that week, the doctor was shocked to see that I had an infection. He prescribed antibiotics, and I returned home and went back to bed, groaning in ever-increasing pain and thinking this *wasn't* what I'd been expecting.

My plan had developed a kink, and I was about to get knocked down.

That night my incision split open, and I saw parts of myself that I never wanted to see. My daughter Vikki and my husband George were with me when it happened. As hard as it was for them, I am extremely grateful they were there, because I was in such misery I could not have coped on my own. They called 911, but even then the problems crowding around me kept kicking and shoving. You see, the paramedics couldn't get the gurney through the door. The stretcher was too wide, and the door was too narrow. So they had to sit me up on a chair and carry me outside.

It would have been an excruciating ordeal even without the complications. But with my incision gaping open and my insides bulging out, the pain was overwhelming.

WHO WOULDN'T SERVE A GOD LIKE THAT?

Maybe about now you're thinking, *What kind of victory-in-Jesus story is THAT to be tellin' me, Thelma? I picked up this book thinking it would inspire me to become closer to the Savior, and you're describin' something that makes me want to lose my lunch? You say you're a believer and you know Jesus can heal you, and yet he let you suffer such trauma? Who would want to serve a Savior like that?*

It's true that sometimes when we need him most we feel far away from God—hurting, alone, forgotten, trampled down by a crowd of problems. Maybe at that point we've given up on ever feeling close to him again. Maybe we feel dirty and unfit, covered with worldly dust that robs us of courage and weakens our faith.

Well, girlfriend, let me tell you: when you find yourself in that kind of ordeal, remember the woman who reached out through the mob to touch the hem of Jesus's cloak. There may have been something in her that wanted to think he had passed her by or forgotten her or turned his back on her. The devil's been wanting us to think that for a long, long time. Ah, but she *knew* better. She knew that even if she didn't feel close to Jesus, even if she couldn't look him in the eye and talk to him face to face, *he* still knew she was there. So she came up behind him and flung out her arm through the raucous crowd, knowing, *If I only touch his cloak, I will be healed.*

And she did. And she was.

Knocked down by blinding pain, horrified by what was happening to me, I felt far from God as the paramedics finally loaded me into the ambulance that night and set off for the hospital with the red lights flashing. That was a very unfamiliar place for Thelma Wells to be. And I'm not just talking about being in the back of the ambulance. I'm talking about feeling far from God.

To explain, let's just climb out of that ambulance for a moment so I can tell you about the lifelong relationship between God and me. You may have heard me say that I grew up in church—and I mean that literally. I was reared by my great-grandparents, and for most of my growing-up years, Granny was in church every day or night of the week—and I went with her: Monday for mission, Tuesday for women's auxiliary, Wednesday for prayer meeting, Thursday for choir rehearsal, and Friday for teachers' meeting. We helped clean the church on Saturdays, and we were back bright and early Sunday mornings.

I guess I thought I knew everything there was to know about God and the church, because when I got to college, I got a little bored and stopped attending services. I had "more urgent" things to do, like study and sleep. Then George and I were married, and Sunday morning was the only time we had to spend together, just the two of us, so we stayed home from church.

I never stopped believing—goodness, no! And I never stopped praying and studying my Bible. But I drifted away from the close relationship I'd always had with God.

This had been going on a few years, when one day I encountered a friend from church who told me a new women's class was being organized, and she not only invited me to attend, she asked me to teach it. She said, "You used to teach, and it was such a wonderful experience, Thelma. I just know you're supposed to come back and teach this class."

I said, "I know you're supposed to get out of my face."

Over the next month I kept running into this woman. She seemed to turn up everywhere I went. To put it short, I'll summarize our long-running dialogue like this:

"Will you teach the class?"

"No!"

"Will you teach the class?"

"No!"

"Will you teach the class?

"OK."

Once I agreed to start teaching again, I got back into researching the Word, and girl, it was like eating a piece of chocolate after being on a decades-long diet. I couldn't get enough of it! I taught that class for ten years, and through that work I became closer than ever to my heavenly Father. Not only was my faith renewed and strengthened by studying his Word, but I also saw it manifested right before my eyes. I learned all over again that he is still the Healer, still the Miracle Worker, still the glorious and omnipotent Lord God Almighty, the same yesterday, today, and forever.

For example, at one point a young woman in the church had leukemia, and she was scheduled to undergo some kind of emergency procedure in the hospital on a Sunday morning. Her mother called the church during Sunday school and asked us to stop and pray for her daughter before the procedure began, and we did exactly that. Later that morning, before the sermon began, the mother called again, crazy with joy, and said, "While you all were praying, they came in to give her one last test before starting the procedure—

and her blood is perfect. They're discharging her. We're leaving the hospital!"

That young woman has not had one symptom of leukemia since that day; her good health is the manifestation of our Jehovah God who is the Healer. God can heal us. I've seen him do it, and each time I've watched a miracle unfold, my faith has grown stronger. I live to love and praise him, and I have felt his powerful presence in my life with every breath I take.

But there I was that night, in the back of that ambulance with my intestines bulging out of my abdomen and pain totally consuming me, and I felt far away from God the Healer, God the Miracle Worker, God my loving Father.

The paramedic who was tending to me as we rushed to the hospital started swabbing my arm with something cold, and I begged him, "Please . . . don't try to find a vein. Please . . . no more pain, no more. Please . . ." Then I struggled to fling out one more prayer through the pain, maybe in the same way that woman in biblical times had stretched out her arm through the crowd: *Oh, Jesus, please! No more! I can't take any more!*

Then, miraculously, before the words had even left my heart, I fell asleep, and the pain ended. I don't remember anything else that happened until at least twenty-four hours later, sometime the next evening.

You may laugh at me now, considering what I was going through then and how far I felt from God, but when I remember that night and how, on that loud and tortuous ambulance ride, Jesus gave me relief, I can't help but think, *Who* wouldn't *serve a Savior like that?*

What She Couldn't Have Known

You see, I know something the woman who believed she would be healed by touching the hem of Jesus's cloak *couldn't* know—because it hadn't happened yet. After my ordeal, I believe I know just a smidgen, just a morsel—just a tee-ninesy bit, as Patsy Clairmont might say—of what Jesus went through when he lay down on that cross to die for me. In my own insignificant way, I have a better under-standing now of the agony Jesus must have felt when he cried out, "My God, my God, why have you forsaken me?" (Matthew 27:46). When I look at the pain and torture he endured for my sake, and then consider the momentary light affliction I went through, I love him more than ever.

I thought I really loved Jesus before, but now I love him more.

I love him more, I love him more, I love him more.

And only now do I believe that my faith comes any-where close to the amazing faith of that woman who knew without a doubt—even before Jesus's crucifixion and the resurrection that were still to come—that he could heal her if she merely touched the hem of the his cloak.

How thankful I am that she knew what she knew—and that her story has been handed down to me two thousand years later.

❦ 3 ❦

Granny's Kind of Gals

Wise . . . women are always learning, always listening for fresh insights.

—Proverbs 18:15 MSG

I GUESS YOU CAN TELL I HAVE A SPECIAL PLACE in my heart for the woman who was healed by merely touching Jesus's cloak. I admire her for many reasons, and one of them is because she reminds me of a very important person in my life, my Granny.

Granny and my great-grandfather—everyone called him Daddy Harrell—brought me into their home when I was just a toddler, and they gave me an upbringing that I cherish today as more precious than gold. Granny was a quiet, humble woman barely known beyond our little back-alley neighborhood. Yet her influence had a profound effect on me, and I've tried my best to carry her character—and her faith—with me wherever I've gone throughout the world.

Granny had the same unfaltering faith of the woman who pushed her way up from the back of the mob to touch the hem of Jesus's garment. Granny knew all about being in the back of the crowd and the back of the bus and the back of the line. As a black woman growing up and living in the South during the era of severe racial segregation, she knew what it was like to have society pass her by and push her down. And yet none of the hardships Granny faced made the slightest dent in her faith. She trusted God for every-thing—*everything!*—and no matter how bad things got, she would sing his praises and keep right on believing.

"God will make a way, girl," she would tell me. That was Granny's response to every difficult situation. She might let herself be discouraged for one split second, but in her heart she knew God would get her through whatever obstacle lay ahead. It probably wouldn't be easy; seems like Granny never got to do anything the easy way. But that didn't faze her.

"God will make a way" was Granny's interpretation of Philippians 4:13, "I can do all things through Christ who strengthens me" (NKJV). And you know what? When you grow up hearing that every day—and seeing it happen—

you start believing it! Again and again, I heard Granny praise God for "making a way" to get us through some kind of hardship or challenge.

For example, after high school I wanted to go to college, but Granny, who worked as a maid for a wealthy family in Dallas, had no money to send me. So I applied to secretarial school instead. My telephone application was accepted, but when I showed up in person to pay the fees and register for classes, I was denied admission because of my race. I retreated home to pour out my anguish to Granny.

"Baby, I know it hurts," she told me, "but I just know the Lord will make a way for you to go to school—and not just secretary's school but real college."

What she was saying seemed impossible. But Granny was one who had studied the Bible all her life, and one of her other favorite verses was Luke 18:27: "What is impossible with men is possible with God." In her mind it all ran together: *God will make a way through the impossible to the possible.*

And the next thing I knew, I was in college. In a special act of kindness, the lady for whom Granny worked as a housemaid paid my tuition until I married; then my husband took over the payments so I could complete my degree.

Granny taught me to stay close to God, and I have.

Honey, it seems like sometimes I'm hanging on to the hem of his cloak and he's *dragging* me through the latest headache or heartache. But I'm not lettin' go, never gonna let go. Because I know he will make a way for me, and when I get through the hard times, I'm gonna be there glorying with him on the other side!

Bravely Speaking Up

Yes, indeed. When I remember the woman who was healed by touching Jesus's garment, I think of my Granny. She spent her life reaching out to Jesus and being helped and healed by his presence. And although I still miss her mightily, even all these years after she moved on to heaven, I love thinking about her up there now, praising her Lord face to face.

There are other women in the Bible who remind me of Granny, as well. Queen Esther is one. Like Granny, Esther was part of an underprivileged minority. She was a Jew, a member of a minority, but amazingly, her own husband, King Xerxes, didn't know it! Persuaded by a no-account shyster named Haman, Xerxes signed an edict that ordered, on a specified date, *all* the Jews in his extensive kingdom were to be annihilated.

Haman had set up Xerxes to become the Hitler of his day.

Esther must have been terrified, worrying what the king would do to her when he found out about her heritage. But then, to compound her fears, her foster father, Mordecai, sent her a message urging her not only to tell the king that she was a Jew but also to speak up for *all* the Jews in the kingdom and beg him to spare her people.

I'm just giving you the *Reader's Digest* version of the story here; there's *so* much more to it, as you'll see when you read the Old Testament book of Esther for yourself. The reason I personally like Esther so much is because she was Granny's kind of gal. The Bible says Esther was beautiful and charming. She "won the favor of everyone who saw her" (2:15), including the king. Well, Granny never won a beauty contest, but to me, she was the most beautiful woman who ever walked the earth, and I don't know a single person who didn't feel the same way about her. Kind to everyone and generous with what little she had, Granny was loved and admired by all who knew her.

But the thing about Esther that reminds me most of Granny was that she was brave. Back in Esther's day, no one was allowed to approach the king unless he or she was invited. If the king did not extend his gold scepter to someone who showed up in his throne room uninvited, that person was put to death!

Esther had *not* been invited. Yet she dared to go. As she gathered courage to make this "surprise" visit, she sent a message to Mordecai, directing him to have all the Jews fast for three days and pray for her. She told him, "I will go to the king, even though it is against the law. And if I perish, I perish" (4:16).

She fasted and prayed along with the rest of the Jews, and then, after three days, she stepped boldly into the king's presence, surely holding her breath to see if he would extend the gold scepter. She had been married to him five years, and she was one of many wives. Maybe she worried that she was no longer his favorite. Maybe she worried that her beauty had faded a bit. We don't know what she thought. But we know what she knew: that she was her people's best hope for avoiding certain death. And surely Mordecai's words were flowing through her mind as she made her move. He had told her, "Who knows but that you have come to royal position for such a time as this?" (Esther 4:14).

So she stepped into the king's throne room, praying that he would smile and extend the gold scepter toward her . . . and he did. But that was just the first hurdle. She still had to tell him she was a Jew—and then beg him to save her people from death.

Maybe you already know how the story ends. In case you don't, I won't spoil it for you. Open your Bible and read it for yourself! I tell you, girlfriend, it's one of the best stories you'll ever read! Best of all, it will inspire you to be bold and speak bravely for what you know is right.

Now, that's not to say you need to be loud-mouthed or pushy. Granny was brave, and she seldom raised her voice for any purpose. She presided over her home and her family with quiet dignity and what I think of as powerful gentleness. The Bible describes Esther's thoughtful preparation for how she would make her request of the king, and in that description you see that the beautiful young queen wanted to make every word count. She didn't whine, she didn't spout off without thinking, and she didn't come across as angry or argumentative. She made her point graciously—over a meal she prepared for the king—and humbly. She said gently, "If it pleases your majesty, grant me my life—this is my petition. And spare my people—this is my request. For I and my people have been sold for destruction and slaughter and annihilation. If we had merely been sold as male and female slaves, I would have kept quiet, because no such distress would justify disturbing the king" (7:3–4).

Like Esther, Granny was a thoughtful and humble person, but she spoke up when she needed to. And I know she had to be as bold as Queen Esther was in the king's throne room when she spoke up to right a wrong early in her career as a domestic. She told me that way back when she was a young woman and started working in the homes of some of the elite families of Dallas, it was not unusual for black housemaids to be approached for sexual favors by the heads of some of those households. It put the young workers in a difficult situation, because these were their employers, and jobs were hard to come by. It was unheard-of for any young African-American domestic to keep her job after rebuffing an employer for making such an approach. All too often, the young woman ended up in a shameful affair, feeling she didn't really have a choice.

Not Granny! The first time her employer surreptitiously sidled up to her and made an inappropriate move, she stepped back from him and said, "I don't know what you think you're doin', Mr. Jones, but you better *never* do it again. I need this job, but I'm not a slut. So if you want me to keep on workin' here, don't do that again!"

He didn't. And word apparently spread that Granny was a good worker and *not* willing to commit adultery to keep her job. She was a brave woman, my Granny.

When we know we're doing right, God helps us do or say what needs to be said. It's up to us, however, to keep our cool and speak bravely in a way that doesn't do more harm than good! Early in my banking career, I had a new boss who came in after I'd been working there awhile. He'd never had an African-American employee, and he wasn't comfortable having me in charge of the bank's bookkeeping department. He set traps for me, leaving sensitive documents lying out to create situations that made me seem careless and put me in a bad light.

But I was smart about what was happening, and one day I called him to my office, and I told him what I knew. I had documented the things I was telling him. I said, "I'll tell you what: I know you don't trust me, but I was here when you got here, and I know more about what's going on than you do. If you want me to leave, I'll leave. I can walk out of here today and start tomorrow at the bank across the street. But as long as I'm here, don't be pullin' any more tricks on me."

He answered, "I'll tell *you* what. You better not ever make a mistake."

I smiled and said, "If you promise me that *you'll* never make a mistake, I'll promise too. I'm human, just like you are."

For three months the man rarely spoke to me and went out of his way to avoid me. Then late one afternoon, just before I was to go home, he called me into his office and said, "I'll admit it. I've tried to trick you every way I could, and I've tried to make you mad. But there's something I like about you: You know what you're doing. You may not agree with me, but you will try the things I ask you to try without a fight. You've got a good team, and you keep your team together. You do your job well, and now I have a reward for you. I'm going to make you a banking officer."

This man who had treated me so badly became the one who first promoted me. Eventually I became a vice president in that bank and went on to have a long and successful career as a banking executive. Isn't that something? And it happened because God granted me the courage to confront someone who had power over me in my career— and then gave me the words to say in that confrontation.

DEBORAH THE DARING

There are several other women in the Bible who remind me of Granny; one of them is Deborah, the prophetess and leader of the Israelites when they were being oppressed by the cruel tyrant Jabin, a king of Canaan (see Judges 4–5). I love Deborah because she reminds me of Granny and also because of what Deborah knew and what I can learn from it today.

And I have to admit there's another reason why I love the story of Deborah: her name means *bee*! And if you know anything about Thelma Wells, you know I *love* bees. I wear some kind of bumblebee jewelry or bee-dazzled clothing every day. My pajamas even have bees on them!

Years ago, I adopted the bumblebee as my own personal logo when I heard that early scientists used to say bumblebees shouldn't be able to fly. Those "experts" said the bumblebee's body is too big and its wings are too short, so, aerodynamically, it should be impossible for the bug to go airborne. But since there are zillions of aerodynamically incorrect bumblebees buzzin' and bumblin' around all over the world, apparently nobody done told that fool it can't fly, as I like to say. (Just bear with me, please, whenever I break into a little down-home dialect now and then; I know better, but it *sounds* so good this way I can't help but indulge myself occasionally.)

I like the bumblebee because I identify with its story. You see, during my life, I've come up against "experts" who've said I couldn't do some things, too, and I've enjoyed nothing more than proving them wrong. So the bumblebee and me, we're tight, as the younger generation might say. (I feel younger just sayin' it, so don't go draggin' out your grammar books and correctin' me.) And I have a personal motto that goes with my personal logo: In Christ, you can *bee* your best.

So when I found out that Deborah means *bee*, I liked her immediately. But when I studied her story and realized what she knew that I could learn from today, well, that was just icing on the cake—or maybe, honey on the hotcakes! Deborah was Granny's kind of gal—and mine too.

The Bible describes an incident that shows how wise Deborah was as she "held court . . . in the hill country of Ephraim" (Judges 4:5). Granny also was a wise counselor; she "held court" in our little back-alley apartment, and later, in the projects. Her judgment was sought by many people in our family and our neighborhood. Granny was a very conservative Christian, but even those whose beliefs clashed with hers found her easy to talk to.

I know now that one of the young women who came to our house often to confide in Granny was living the lesbian lifestyle. She talked to Granny about it, and I'm sure Granny didn't approve. Yet she was able to counsel this young woman gently, in a way that didn't push her away but kept her coming back for more of Granny's kind company and careful listening. And eventually the woman realized the error of her ways and came out of that lifestyle.

Likewise, the Israelites came to Deborah for wise counsel and sound judgments. But Deborah wasn't just wise;

she was also brave. Her bravery came from what she knew: that God was with her and that he would guide her in using her brains and her resources to do his will.

For twenty years, the Israelites had been "cruelly oppressed" by the Canaan king Jabin, whose army, commanded by the powerful Sisera, included "nine hundred iron chariots," which were probably considered the weapons of mass destruction of their day. Deborah wasn't afraid of that army and its chariots, however. She called in a man named Barak and relayed to him God's directions to lead ten thousand Israelites to battle against Sisera.

Maybe you think Barak answered the little lady confidently, "Whatever you say, honey. I'll take care of it." But instead he whined, "If you go with me, I will go; but if you don't go with me, I won't go" (Judges 4:8).

So Deborah pulled on her Superwoman cape—or maybe it was a cloak, the kind that would be worn by the Savior hundreds of years later when another miracle was needed— and she set off with her prissy-pants general to conquer the enemy's army. She had the help of another brave woman, Jael, as she did so. Jael drove a tent peg through a villain's head to do what needed to be done (see Judges 4:17–22)!

I was a lot like Barak when I was growing up. I wanted Granny beside me whenever I set off to conquer the world.

I'm not sure what I thought a spindly little old black woman in precarious health could do to protect me from whatever it was "out there" that frightened me, but throughout my childhood, I always felt braver if Granny came with me. She was my rock, and Jesus was hers. We faced some difficult challenges, but just like Barak did when he had Deborah with him, we prevailed.

TAKING THE BLAME FOR SOMEONE ELSE'S FOOLISHNESS

Another Old Testament woman, Abigail, differed from Granny in that Abigail had a wicked and foolish husband— in fact, her husband Nabal's name meant *fool*. There was *nothing* foolish or wicked about Daddy Harrell. Like Granny, he was one of the wisest ones I've ever known.

But the thing about Abigail that makes her Granny's kind of gal was that she had the gift of being able to defuse explosive situations. Granny and Abigail could say a few words and ease the wrath of someone who was out for vengeance.

Abigail did that when foolish Nabal insulted David before David became king. Nabal refused to pay David what he owed him, and David was furious at the injustice. Abigail had nothing to do with Nabal's ridiculous and thoughtless actions, but when she heard what had happened, she knew David would be justified in killing her husband and destroying their entire household. Risking her own life, she hurried to intercept David before he could carry out his revenge. First Samuel 25:23–24 records how she passionately took the blame for her foolish husband's actions.

> When Abigail saw David, she quickly got off her donkey and bowed down before David with her face to the ground. She fell at his feet and said: "My lord, let the blame be on me alone. Please let your servant speak to you; hear what your servant has to say."

Abigail went on to praise David and remind him that he represented the Lord in the battles he fought and that someday when he was "ruler over Israel" he would regret the vengeful killing he was about to enact.

Abigail's plea shows us that she knew something we would do well to heed today. She already knew what David's own son Solomon (who wasn't even born yet) would write many years later: "A gentle answer turns away wrath" (Proverbs 15:1).

Abigail had courage, grit, and good sense. And so did

Granny. Like Abigail, Granny sometimes intercepted with "a gentle answer" my plans for revenge after someone had hurt my feelings or insulted me with thoughtless words or deeds. Granny in her sweet wisdom would say, "Girl, you just get along 'bout your own business. Don't waste your time on her. She's not worth ruinin' your reputation, and that's what will happen if you do something bad back at her. Let God deal with her. You just think about Thelma and what Jesus wants Thelma to do. Let your light shine, girl. Let it shine for him, and he'll take care of you."

That was the kind of advice she gave me while I was enrolled in a business class taught by a woman who refused to recognize my presence in the class. All the other students were called upon to read their work aloud, but throughout the whole semester that teacher never once called on me. When I asked her privately why she was ignoring me, she said, "I've ever taught a negress, and I'm not about to start now."

Well, I stormed home and poured out my anger and wrath to Granny. I wanted to report that teacher, get her in trouble, slash her tires, toilet-paper her lawn, and put chewing gum in her hair. Girl, I wanted to hurt her like she had hurt me!

But Granny advised otherwise. "Thelma, you just go on

and learn from her," Granny said. "You learn everything you can from her, and that will be the best revenge."

I had to admit that, except for her attitude toward me, the woman was a talented teacher. So I did just what Granny said, and I soaked up every bit of knowledge I could from that woman—I even signed up for the advanced course she taught the next semester! At the end of the year, I waited for her after class and told her, "Miss Smith, you may not have wanted to teach me anything, but you did. I learned a lot from you. I just wanted you to know that."

Yes, Granny and Abigail were a lot alike. And both of them felt the goodness of God's love rewarding them for their devotion. Granny lived a long, productive life. Abigail . . . well, a short time later, after Nabal died of a stroke, Abigail married David!

The Wisdom to Seek Out Wisdom

The queen of Sheba was one of Granny's kind of gals, even though they came from different ends of the social ladder of wealth and privilege. She reminds me of Granny because she earnestly sought wisdom. She loved to learn, and so did Granny. Granny read and re-read her Bible until it was just about worn out . . . and she just kept right on reading it.

Sometimes I think she soaked up God's Word just by feeling its familiar weight in her gnarled and rugged hands.

The queen of Sheba heard about a wise man called Solomon. She heard about his sayings and his wisdom, and she longed to sit at his feet and learn from him. She loaded up her caravan and journeyed from her country in Arabia to Jerusalem, where Solomon lived. She begged to sit at Solomon's feet and listen, and when she did she was mesmerized, overcome by what he taught her. She told King Solomon, "It was a true report which I heard in my own land about your words and your wisdom. However I did not believe the words until I came and saw with my own eyes; and indeed the half was not told me. Your wisdom and prosperity exceed the fame of which I heard" (1 Kings 10:6–7 NKJV).

The queen of Sheba was hungry for the wisdom Solomon possessed, and she came a long way—later Jesus would say she came "from a far corner of the earth" (Matthew 12:41 MSG)—to seek it out. She gave Solomon many, many gifts in gratitude for sharing his wisdom with her, and later she gave him even more gifts. We can't help but believe that the queen took home the wisdom Solomon gave her and revolutionized her nation. Granny may not have changed the face of *her* nation, but she certainly impacted the heart of at least one little girl: me. And all these years later, I carry her love of God's wisdom with me wherever I go.

THE INSIGHTS OF ANNA

Anna reminds me of Granny because she, too, was very wise. What she knew was nothing short of miraculous. She knew exactly who Jesus was long before other members of that community—and the world—discovered the Messiah in their midst. Anna's "insider knowledge" reminds me so much of Granny. She knew Jesus like nobody else, and she saw Jesus in the unlikeliest of people.

When Mary and Joseph brought the baby Jesus to the temple to be consecrated, they were first seen by a devout man named Simeon who'd been told by God that he would not die until he had seen the Messiah. Simeon was drawn to the temple courtyard the day Mary and Joseph brought Jesus there, and when he saw the baby, he cried out, "You now dismiss your servant in peace. For my eyes have seen your salvation" (Luke 2:29–30).

Mary and Joseph were amazed at Simeon's words, and then, as if to underscore what had happened, Anna appeared next on the scene. Luke 2:36–38 describes what happened:

There was a prophetess, Anna. . . . She was very old; she had lived with her husband seven years after her marriage, and then was a widow until she was eighty-four. She never left the temple but worshiped night and day, fasting and praying. Coming up to them at that very moment, she gave thanks to God and spoke about the child to all who were looking forward to the redemption of Jerusalem.

Anna could see the Messiah in that sweet baby's face, and she told others what she had seen. Granny did the same. She could see Jesus in people others might have turned away from. When someone created a poor impression or was unpleasant to be around, Granny would say, "You've gotta look *through* 'em to see Jesus, girl." Somehow, Granny had a way of seeing people's true heart—even when their behavior made you wonder if they had one!

She also taught me to discern the real gospel message even when it's buried in glitz and glamour. I've been blessed to be in some churches that have had highly skilled pastors who present spellbinding sermons and lead over-the-top worship services. Granny's word of wisdom has helped me stay focused during these dynamic services and put the powerful preacher in the proper perspective. Granny knew it was easy to get so caught up in the personality of a dynamic, engaging human being that the simple teachings of the only holy One, Jesus Christ, can be neglected. She helped me learn to sort through all the trappings of an elaborate service and focus my attention solely on God and his Son. This same practice also keeps me from being disappointed when a preacher is less skillful in presenting his message.

Just as Anna somehow knew that the Messiah was being carried into the temple that day as a helpless infant, I try to see God's promises being lived out in the world around me, as I do my best to live them out as well.

THE GIRLS IN THE GRAVEYARD

And finally, let me briefly mention another biblical character who was definitely Granny's kind of gal: Mary Magdalene. I don't need a lot of room to tell you why she reminds me of Granny because Mary Mag's story is well-known and her love of the Lord was profound. Mary Mag was also brave. Others ran away during that terrible afternoon when Jesus was crucified, but Mary Mag and a handful of others stayed. She wasn't afraid to be seen mourning the death of the One she loved and others despised. And she wasn't afraid to go to the dark tomb where his body was taken after it was removed from the cross.

Granny wasn't afraid of doing things other people shied away from, and she wouldn't have hesitated one moment to go to Jesus's tomb that Sunday morning, no matter how spooky the graveyard seemed in the pre-dawn darkness and no matter how strong the odor of decaying flesh might have been. She would have been there with her bag of ointments and basket of herbs to anoint her dear Lord's body. I have no doubt of it.

But the real reason I think of Granny whenever I recall the story of that resurrection morning is that, when Jesus spoke to Mary Magdalene outside the tomb, he told her to go and tell the others he was alive (see John 20:17–18).

Mary Magdalene ran to the disciples and proclaimed, "I have seen the Lord!" And my Granny did the same thing. With every breath on every day of her life, she lived out that proclamation to all who knew her.

BECOMING GRANNY'S KIND OF GAL

The biblical women in this chapter were focused in their faith, brave and wise, and they knew the Lord in ways that caused others to notice. I think of Granny when I study their stories. I want to be like them. I want to know what they knew—and show that I know it by the way I live.

❦ 4 ❦

The Maids and Matrons Who Molded Moses

The Israelis were . . . in deep trouble because of
their slavery, and weeping bitterly before the LORD.
. . . Looking down upon them, he knew that the
time had come for their rescue.

—Exodus 2:23, 25 TLB

NO WONDER MOSES TURNED OUT TO BE SUCH A magnificent man of God. His life was saved—and then molded—by some extraordinarily wise, clever, and courageous women.

We know that Moses's birth father was Amram (see Exodus 6:20 and Numbers 26:59), and although we assume he had no role in Moses's upbringing, we can also assume he was a God-fearing man, a member of the family of Levites. Moses's adoptive grandfather, on the other hand, was a hard-hearted scoundrel. He was Pharaoh, the king of Egypt, who sent out a decree that Moses was to be killed at birth. Well, not Moses specifically, but all the Hebrew baby boys. Pharaoh thought the Jews he had enslaved were getting too populous—and thus too powerful. So he set out to commit infanticide.

His first attempt at this mass murder was to instruct Hebrew midwives Shiphrah and Puah to kill all baby boys at birth. We don't know whether they attended Moses's mother, Jochebed, when she gave birth, but we do know they "feared God and did not do what the king of Egypt had told them to do; they let the boys live" (Exodus 1:17). So right there, before or at Moses's birth, two strong, God-fearing women had an impact on his life. If they didn't actually deliver Moses, they surely inspired his mother to be brave and take steps to protect her son's life.

When Pharaoh asked the midwives why there were still so many little Hebrew boys cooing and gurgling out in Slave Town, they feigned innocence, saying, "Hebrew women are not like Egyptian women; they are vigorous and give birth before the midwives arrive" (Exodus 1:19).

Don't you just love that? Those silver-tongued heroines had the perfect answer for the vicious Pharaoh; their words protected the Hebrew babies and saved their own necks from the noose. You get the feeling they might even have offered to go into greater depth about the birthing process, but Pharaoh, being a man and all, maybe got a little squeamish and didn't want to hear it.

Instead, Pharaoh ordered *all* the people to join him in his conspiracy of murder. He said they all had to throw every Hebrew boy baby into the Nile when he was born.

It's hard to imagine that Pharaoh expected to see the bodies of dead babies floating on the river, but that's what he ordered. We don't know how or to what extent this decree was carried out, but we can imagine the agony it generated. Did the Egyptians raid the homes of new mothers, grab the infant sons from their arms, and hurl the tiny babes into the river? Did the parents themselves, fearful that they would be killed and thus leave their older children orphaned, drown their own baby boys? The mere thought of it moves me to tears.

We don't know what really happened in those other Hebrew families, but we do know that when Jochebed gave birth to "an unusually beautiful baby" (Exodus 2:2 TLB), she did *not* throw him into the Nile. No, she couldn't do that. Instead, "she hid him for three months" (Exodus 2:2).

Any mother who's tried to keep an infant quiet for one hour during a church service can appreciate how hard it must have been for Jochebed to hide her baby boy for *three months*. Remember, *all* the people were under Pharaoh's decree to throw the Hebrew baby boys in the Nile. So we have to assume that anyone who helped Jochebed keep her secret was just as vulnerable as she was. Anyone who defied the decree could come under the harsh judgment of the king.

How did Jochebed cover his cries? How did she do his laundry without someone noticing? How did she answer the questions of those who had known she was pregnant? Did she simply dress the baby in pink and hope nobody was looking during diaper changes? Can you imagine the sleepless nights, the long days, this woman endured to protect her son? And how interesting that her husband is not mentioned in any of this narrative. You have to wonder, was Jochebed hiding from him too?

We have to hope that, somewhere, sometime in his long life, Moses heard and appreciated the brave courage of his determined mother—and also of the brave midwives who, even if they didn't specifically save Moses's life, saved many others. I hope he knew what his mother went through for those three long months as, in every minute of every one of those ninety or so days, she risked her life to save his.

Whether or not Moses knew, *I* know, thousands of years later, and the bravery of those women who gave Moses his start in life gives me courage to face the challenges that start up in mine. Thinking about their story, you almost wonder if they knew, right from the beginning, that this baby was destined for greatness . . .

THE PEASANT AND THE PRINCESS

Finally Jochebed must have decided, reluctantly, that she couldn't keep her baby boy a secret any longer. Imagine the tears that dropped into that little basket of bulrushes she wove to cradle her son. Imagine how her heart pounded as she bundled him into the basket and set it onto the mighty river. What do you suppose she wished for as she gently pushed it away from the river bank and into the current? Her best hope was probably for something impossible to happen, something that would have to be nothing less than a miracle. Everyone in the kingdom was under the Pharaoh's decree to throw all the baby boys into the

Nile, so Jochebed needed someone who was very brave—even braver than she was—to rescue her baby and defy Pharaoh's decree.

Who could possibly be that brave? Only someone who didn't fear Pharaoh.

And who, in all the kingdom, wouldn't be afraid of a ruthless ruler who held the power of life or death over each of his subjects? Why, Daddy's little princess, of course!

Yes, indeed. It was Pharaoh's own daughter who rescued Jochebed's son from the river. And she was no dimwit. She knew exactly what the situation was as soon as she'd sent one of her slave girls to fetch the basket she'd spotted on the water. "She opened it and saw the baby. He was crying, and she felt sorry for him. 'This is one of the Hebrew babies,' she said" (Exodus 2:6).

Now comes the strangest part of the whole story, if you ask me. It turns out that the baby's big sister, Miriam, had been secretly watching the basket float down the Nile. We don't know how old Miriam was; we don't know if this was Miriam's own idea or if her mother suggested it. And we don't know if Miriam had already planned what she would say if and when someone plucked the basket from the river, or if her mother had coached her. There's so much we don't know—and so much we have to assume.

For instance, we can be pretty certain that Miriam was frightened when she approached the princess. She would probably have known the identity of the wealthy woman surrounded by slave girls who'd come to bathe in the river. As a Hebrew, Miriam herself was a slave, but we assume she was much younger and didn't have the high rank of those who attended the princess. By stepping forward, she might open herself to suspicious questioning that could force her to reveal the whole story of how her mother had defied the Pharaoh's edict for three long months. Maybe she would even be forced to lead the royal group to her home, where her mother—or both parents—might be arrested.

Yes, young Miriam's heart was surely in her throat as she stepped from her hiding place and asked the princess, "Shall I go and get one of the Hebrew women to nurse the baby for you?" (Exodus 2:7).

Did the princess peer into the young girl's eyes and leave the obvious truth unsaid? We've already said that Pharaoh's daughter was smart enough to know instantly that the baby in the basket was one of the Hebrew baby boys who was supposed to have been killed at birth. Did someone this smart really think Miriam was an innocent bystander who just happened to be nearby at the river when the basket was discovered, and who also just happened to know a woman who was already nursing a female infant? (It had to be a female because all the boy infants were supposed to have been drowned, right?)

Whatever the truth was, an amazing thing happened as the result of that encounter. Pharaoh's daughter agreed to Miriam's suggestion, and the girl ran off and got her mother. When Jochebed stood before the princess, she heard what must have been an incredible order. "Take this baby and nurse him for me, and I will pay you" (v. 9), Pharaoh's daughter told her.

It's too bad we don't have a photograph or some other kind of picture to commemorate that unlikely gathering of three women—Jochebed, Miriam, and the Pharaoh's daughter—who unintentionally conspired to rear one of the founders of our faith. Standing there on the banks of the Nile, they surely had no idea how the baby in their midst would someday change their world.

The Bible tells this part of Moses's story so succinctly, we have to use our imaginations to fill in the gaps. We can't know for sure what these women knew about each other, but we can be sure of one thing: all three of them had compassionate hearts. They stared into that basket woven of bulrushes, and their hearts melted at the sight of the beautiful baby boy nestled there.

It's been said that Moses's story proves how precious every little life is. Moses was an adopted child who grew up and changed the course of history. Neither the mother who gave him up nor the mother who adopted him could have known that the baby boy in the basket was destined for greatness. But somehow they knew that saving him was the right thing to do.

Isn't it amazing who God uses to carry out his plans—and how he puts the unlikeliest people together? You never know who he might use next. It might be me. Or you. He might even put us together somehow to manage something miraculous!

This book is a look at what some women of the Bible knew—and we can't be sure of what Jochebed, Miriam, and the Pharaoh's daughter knew that day beside the Nile. But *we* know today that they were living out God's plan for their lives, whether or not they recognized that fact.

Growing Up Great

There's a lot we don't know about Moses's childhood. The Bible tells us that Pharaoh's daughter told Moses's mother to "take this baby and nurse him for me, and I will pay you" (Exodus 2:9). Jochebed did that, and in the next verse we're told simply, "When the child grew older, she took him to Pharaoh's daughter and he became her son. She named him Moses, saying, 'I drew him out of the water'" (v. 10).

We don't know what kind of home life Moses had. But as a prince growing up in the palace, we have to assume he had the finest education, the best teachers, the greatest opportunities, and the broadest experiences. We might be tempted to think that children who grow up as princes and princesses are spoiled and shallow, incapable of assuming responsibility for making their own way and disinterested in anything but themselves. Let's be honest. We see a lot of that in our culture today among the offspring of celebrities and wealthy parents. Sometimes those who have the greatest resources for doing good end up wasting everything, including their own health and future.

Moses easily could have turned out that way too. But he didn't, perhaps because of the upbringing he received—the loving start from his birth mother and maybe the inspiring guidance from his adoptive mother (and perhaps even his grandfather the Pharaoh) throughout his growing-up years.

We don't know exactly *how* Moses's life was molded during his youth, but we do know how he turned out. Someone during Moses's childhood must have taught him to have a compassionate heart and an intelligent mind, and we can't help but think that the woman who reared him, the Pharaoh's daughter, played a part in bringing about that result. Moses apparently grew up knowing who he was, a Jew rather than an Egyptian. We have to assume his adoptive mother didn't try to disguise him or hide his heritage from him. We assume this because Exodus 2:11–12 says, "One day, after Moses had grown up, he went out to where *his own people* were and watched them at their hard labor. He saw an Egyptian beating a Hebrew, *one of his own people*. Glancing this way and that and seeing no one, he killed the Egyptian and hid him in the sand" (emphasis mine).

That episode brought an end to Moses's life of wealth and privilege. And because we're looking at this story from the female perspective, we can't help but think his adoptive mother was hurt by Moses's grown-up rejection of her when he "refused to be known as the son of Pharaoh's daughter" (Hebrews 11:24). And surely her heart ached for him when he abruptly disappeared from Egypt, fleeing from his adoptive grandfather, the Pharaoh, who heard what had happened and "tried to kill Moses" (Exodus 2:15).

If ever you start thinking that God can't use you because of your background—because of who you are, how you were reared, or what you have or haven't done during your life— think again! If you think you're too poor or too worldly to be useful to the Creator as he carries out his plan of salvation, think of the unlikely heroines who saved a little baby boy from an imperial decree of death and, by doing so, changed the face of history.

THE FEISTY GO-GETTER

Moses fled to Midian, and eventually he married a woman named Zipporah. I love this woman, and I love what she knew. I envision Zipporah as a feisty go-getter, a woman who worked day and night, who loved her family and was especially close to her father, Jethro. She ended up in an interracial marriage, a mixture of cultures. She was a black Ethiopian woman married to a Hebrew man, Moses. And she was determined to learn about his culture and understand his heart.

They lived together many years, and I like to think that sometimes while Moses was out there tending Jethro's sheep, maybe Zipporah brought him something to eat and sat by the fire with him. Maybe he told her about the Hebrew culture and its traditions, including the ritual of circumcising infant boys when they were eight days old.

Later, when Moses reluctantly heeded God's instructions to return to Egypt to free the Israelites, Zipporah and their two sons went right along with him. But the strangest thing happened as they traveled. Right after God told Moses his plan for confronting Pharaoh about releasing the Israelites, God became angry at Moses. This story is a difficult Bible passage to understand, at least for me, but from studying several discussions of it, I've come to believe that Zipporah knew what the problem was and perhaps Moses was pretending to be clueless. Apparently he had not followed one of the strongest traditions of his own culture and had failed to circumcise at least one of his sons, and now the boy was well beyond infanthood.

Zipporah, though she wasn't a Jew, knew what was wrong, and when she saw that Moses was too scared or too squeamish or too *whatever* to make things right, she took it upon herself to do what had to be done to save her husband from God's wrath. Here's how Exodus 4:24–26 describes the gruesome scene:

> On the way to Egypt, at a place where Moses and his family had stopped for the night, the Lord confronted him and was about to kill him. But Moses' wife, Zipporah, took a flint knife and circumcised her son. She touched his feet with the foreskin and said, "Now you are a bridegroom of

blood to me." (When she said "a bridegroom of blood," she was referring to the circumcision.) After that, the Lord left him alone. (NLT)

Mercy! Can you imagine how upset Zipporah was, having to do something so hurtful to her son . . . to save her husband? But she knew there was a terrible problem between Moses and the Lord, and she knew what had to be done. She may have embarrassed Moses by doing what he should have done. But embarrassment is better than death. We can learn from this strong-willed woman who crossed cultures and stood by her man, even when he couldn't stand up for his own beliefs.

Now, I'm not saying my husband and I came from different cultures, but we do have some differences in opinion, and sometimes that causes a little friction, if you know what I mean. One of our differing opinions concerns gambling. My husband loves the casino. One of his requirements if we go on a vacation is that there must be a casino.

I know a lot of you out there are raising your eyebrows and tsk-tsking that Thelma Wells's husband is a gambler. Zipporah may have had the same reaction from her family and friends when she married a Jew. I assure you George is a good Christian man, a devoted husband, father, and grandfather, and wonderful nurturer to everyone in his family. Gambling isn't a problem for him. He doesn't do it every day. But if he gets a chance two or three times a year to spend some time in a casino, he takes it.

That means whenever the Women of Faith conference goes to Las Vegas or Shreveport, George comes along. I don't disapprove of George spending time in the casinos. On the other hand, if I don't have time to lay out the whole picture, as I'm doing here, I don't advertise the fact either. Believe it or not, some people, including Christians, like to make snap judgments about someone's spirituality based on one little characteristic.

One time Women of Faith had been in Las Vegas, and George was with me. We were at the airport, heading home. I was sitting with some of the other speakers and staff in the gate area, where they had conveniently placed a one-armed bandit, or whatever the thing was, and George was having a great time playing it. They called for us to board, and everybody lined up . . . except George. He's still over there feedin' that thing quarters, puh-*ching*! puh-*ching*! puh-*ching*!

I called to him as quietly and respectfully as I could, trying not to attract the attention of the one hundred fifty or so other people in the gate area, but he was so absorbed in all those bells and whistles, he didn't even look up. I went ahead and got on the plane, thinking he would eventually realize it was time to go.

Because of all my frequent flyer miles, I'm often lucky enough to get upgraded to a first class seat at the front of the plane, and that day I settled into my seat and waited for George to join me. The other passengers filed past me, looking for their seats. No George. Through the plane's open doorway, I could hear that one-armed bandit still binging and dinging: puh-*ching*! puh-*ching*! puh-*ching*!

Finally, when the aisle cleared and the flight attendants were closing up the overhead bins and preparing for takeoff, I lost it. I wiggled out of my seat, marched down the aisle, stood in the doorway of the plane and hollered as loud as I could, "GEORGE WELLS! GET ON THIS PLANE RIGHT NOW!"

Then I turned around and shuffled back to my seat, keeping my eyes on the floor so I couldn't see the shocked faces of my fellow passengers. As I settled back into my seat, the flight attendant brought me a glass of water, probably thinking my throat was dry after all that yellin'. "Ms. Wells, I sure did enjoy the Women of Faith conference yesterday," she said as I gulped down the liquid.

I nearly spewed the water all over the person in front of me. "Oh! You *know* me?" I said. "Oh! I'm so embarrassed."

"Oh, don't be," she said, laughing warmly. "This is so funny. And, you know, we've all got *stuff* to deal with. It just makes us human."

So now you now: George and Thelma Wells, just like Moses and Zipporah, are totally, terribly human.

THE DAUGHTER OF DELEGATION

Here's another thing I believe we can learn from Zipporah: the importance of delegating. I could be wrong; I'm reading between the lines of Exodus 18, which doesn't give us details of how things unfolded. But I believe Zipporah should be credited with coming up with the idea for the Hebrews' first corporate structure. I believe she suggested that structure so her husband could get some rest.

Moses led the children of Israel out of Egypt, and Zipporah was with him. But after a while he sent her and their sons home to her father. And I suspect that while she was home, she told her father that Moses needed help. While the Jews were out there in the desert, Moses was trying to be chief cook and bottle washer—judge, jury, jailer, and everything else—for those hundreds of thousands of people. Surely he was exhausted.

I believe Zipporah again saw what was happening and

urged her father to intervene. I can imagine her telling Jethro, "Daddy, my husband is leading several hundred thousand people through the desert, and he's trying to tend to each and every one of them. He's stressed to the max, and he just can't keep on going the way he's going now. I want you to tell him for me—he'll listen to you—I want you to tell him he needs to develop a delegation plan. He needs to organize some teams to handle the minor judgments and decisions that have to made. He can't be responsible for making every decision that has to be made. He can't be Judge Judy and preside over Traffic Court, too. Daddy, I want you to figure out a plan so Moses can have some rest."

The Bible doesn't tell us where Jethro got the idea for what he later proposed to Moses. But I like to think it came from Zipporah. Here's what happened when she and her father rejoined Moses in the desert:

Moses took his seat to serve as judge for the people, and they stood around him from morning till evening. When his father-in-law saw all that Moses was doing for the people, he said, "What is this you are doing for the people? Why do you alone sit as judge, while all these people stand around you from morning till evening?"

Moses answered him, "Because the people come to me to seek God's will. Whenever they have a dispute, it is brought to me, and I decide between the parties and inform them of God's decrees and laws."

Moses' father-in-law replied, "What you are doing is not good. You and these people who come to you will only wear yourselves out. The work is too heavy for you; you cannot handle it alone. Listen now to me and I will give you some advice, and may God be with you. You must be the people's representative before God and bring their disputes to him. Teach them the decrees and laws, and show them the way to live and the duties they are to perform. But select capable men from all the people— men who fear God, trustworthy men who hate dishonest gain—and appoint them as officials over thousands, hundreds, fifties and tens. Have them serve as judges for the people at all times, but have them bring every difficult case to you; the simple cases they can decide themselves. That will make your load lighter, because they will share it with you. If you do this and God so commands, you will be able to stand the strain, and all these people will go home satisfied."

Moses listened to his father-in-law and did everything he said. (Exodus 18:13–24)

I choose to believe that this system of delegating came from Zipporah through her father, Jethro, to Moses. And for that reason, I choose to think of Zipporah as the daughter of delegation. Her idea shows us modern businesswomen, managers, even parents, the importance of delegating jobs to others.

Sure, we all fall prey occasionally to the idea that if you want something done right you have to do it yourself. But realizing we *can't* do it all ourselves is a positive step, because when we decide to delegate, we see the importance of sharing our knowledge, of training those we want to assist us. We teach . . . and then we release them to do the job.

So parents teach their children when they're very young to assist with the chores at home. They can take the trash out, wash the dishes, hang up their clothes, pick up their toys. Parents can do that—it's the art of delegation. In the workplace there are people who are more skilled at certain tasks than the manager is. A good manager seeks out those people who can be trusted to do good work and make the manager look good!

There was a time when, like Moses, I tried to do it all. But as my ministries grew and my speaking engagements increased, I quickly became overwhelmed. Now I have trusted coworkers (who also happen to be my close friends, which makes it even better) who not only do the things I used to do, they also have skills to do things I can't do, like updating our Web page and creating Power Point presentations and designing attractive mailing pieces.

I believe Zipporah knew Moses was headed for an early death due to too much work and responsibility, and once again she intervened to save him—this time from himself. Moses may never have suspected that the system his father-in-law suggested was actually his wife's idea, as I believe. But you know, we women have intuition about these things. Sometimes we *know* things, even when there's no way to know it. Isn't that right?

Whose Life Are You Impacting?

In this chapter we've looked at a Bible character everyone knows—Moses—but our focus has been, not on the man himself, but on the lesser-known characters—the women—who impacted and molded his life. What powerful lessons they teach us! And perhaps most important is the lesson that God can and will use whomever he chooses to fulfill his purpose, no matter how unlikely or how unfit those characters may seem when considered as possibilities for godly service. A family of slaves . . . a baby in a basket . . . a pagan princess

. . . a wife of the "wrong" background . . . who could be more unlikely to work together to mold the man who would bring about the mass exodus of a nation from cruel captivity?

Think of these women the next time you're feeling that your life seems insignificant. The next time you're stuck at home raising young children or you're out in the business world overwhelmed with work. Learn from what these women knew and did. Recognize that your "insignificant" work may be part of God's greater plans—plans he designed "to prosper you and not to harm you, plans to give you hope and a future" (Jeremiah 29:11).

⊱ 5 ⊰

Learning from Broken Hearts

The nights of crying your eyes out give way to days of laughter.

—Psalm 30:5 MSG

WHEN COMPLICATIONS AROSE AFTER MY HYSTER-ectomy, I went back to the hospital in an ambulance—and all my plans for the holidays and the next year of my life went out the window.

Cook a family feast for Christmas? Forget it.

Celebrate the New Year with church friends? Not happening.

Teach a weeklong class in January for Master's International Divinity School? Class canceled.

Lead the weekend retreat in February for my Daughters of Zion mentoring program? Sisters, y'all just go on ahead and retreat without me.

Show up in Fort Lauderdale for the 2006 Women of Faith National Conference? You've gotta be kidding.

About the only plan I was able to fulfill was my pajama plan. Before I had surgery, I didn't like pajamas. To be honest, they were way too staid and boring for me, being the fashionable sexpot that I am! I was more into negligees and girly stuff, if you know what I mean. But one day, long before I knew I had to have surgery, I happened upon a whole rack of pajamas during a shopping trip, and they really appealed to me.

If you know Thelma Wells at all, you know how I like stuff on my clothes—bumblebees and sparkly things. Well, these pajamas had little sequins around the bottom of the pants, and the tops had little sequins and little satin ribbons. I looked at those pajamas and thought, *They are TOO cute! I wouldn't mind walking around the house with these on, even if they are pajamas.* I bought seven pairs of them!

And then I didn't wear them. They were, after all, pajamas—and I don't like pajamas. I decided maybe I would give them as gifts. But I didn't do that either. Then, several months later, when I had to have surgery, I thought up the pajama plan. I knew my daughters and my friends would be helping me during my recovery (which of course I expected to be very brief), and I didn't want them to see all the sexy negligees in my dresser drawer. I didn't want to shock them. (Let's face it. No daughter wants to think of her mother wearing anything that might have come from Victoria's Secret, let alone the Fredericks of Hollywood kind of stuff that filled my dresser drawers.) So I took out the sexy negligees and put my bling-bling pajamas in there, along with some flowing caftans and lots of cute socks. I pictured myself saying to my friends or my daughters who would be helping me after I'd showered each morning, "Sugar, look over there in that drawer and get me those green pajamas or those black pajamas."

Then they would see the pajamas and think, *Oh, this looks just like Thelma, so fun, yet so modest.*

Of all the plans I had for the first half of 2006, my pajama plan was the only one that came to fruition. And then when I did start wearing my new pajamas, I wore them a long, long, *long* time—way longer than I ever *planned* to wear them or wanted to wear them.

The rest of my looking-slick-while-sick plan was a total failure. For instance, I also bought some bling-bling warm-up suits to wear in the hospital after the surgery, thinking I would be a well-heeled-while-healing hostess reigning graciously over groups of visitors who dropped by my hotel, er, hospital room. I sat my children down before I left for the hospital the first time and said, "You all are to keep my nails looking good and my feet looking cute. Don't let my heels get rusty with calluses, and don't let my polish get chipped. You rub me down with sweet-smellin' stuff and put some makeup on my face and make sure my hair looks good. Put a little perfume on me, and keep my room clean. Do you hear me?"

I had my little makeup case packed and everything they would need to keep me suitably turned out. And do you think after my surgery I cared one whit about any of that? My girls told me they did just as I had instructed them, but I didn't know—or care—whether or not they did it.

I do remember puckering my lips one time when a friend came to visit, indicating to her that I needed some Carmex. My lips were so dry! But my friend didn't know what Carmex was, and baby, she opened that little can and put that stuff *alllllll* over my whole face. She didn't know it's supposed to be for the lips. She greased me up so good, when I tried to open my eyes, my eyelids pushed up a big wad of Carmex all the way to my eyebrows!

ADVANCING THROUGH ADVERSITY

Looking back, I have to laugh at all the plans I made for my doctor, my family, and my body to follow in getting through my surgical adventure in an efficient and satisfactory manner. My experience brings me new appreciation for that little quip that says, "If you want to make God laugh, tell him your plans." I had my whole year planned out, right down to the nail polish and pajamas I'd soon be wearing. And if I'd listened closely as I formulated those plans, I probably could have heard God laughing.

When things don't work out the way we plan . . . when we're handed loss while we're hoping for luck . . . when our rewarding work suddenly collapses into rubble . . . when someone or something we love is taken from us . . . the light goes out of our lives. We're lost, not understanding why calamity has swept through our lives and dumped us in some dark place far from hope. We think of what we had planned and what has happened instead, and our hearts break open with cries and questions. *Why, Lord? Why me? Why now? Why this? Why my child* or *my husband* or *my loved one?*

The truth is, we may never know, this side of eternity, why God sometimes lets us stumble forlornly through the valley of the shadow of death. But if we're smart, we'll find the advantage in every adversity: in that dark valley, we'll reach out to God and pull ourselves closer to him as he reaches out to comfort and encourage us.

I had planned a few weeks of recovery following a major but rather routine surgical procedure. Instead I was essentially housebound for more than six months and disabled for several months after that. I endured pain like I had never known before (and hope never to know again!). I had to give up all the entertaining, rewarding, and (I thought) essential events and activities I had scheduled in great detail.

For all I had given up, all I had lost, I grieved and cried and threw myself long, drawn-out pity parties.

And when all that gnashing of teeth and wearing of pajamas was done, when I settled into the quiet routine of being home all day . . . all week . . . all month, I found the advantage in my adversity. I found myself growing closer, ever closer, to my Savior, my Lord, my God.

When I knew I was going to be home all day with nothing "important" going on, I didn't have to rush through my morning prayers. I didn't have to read one chapter of my Bible then shove it in my computer bag before rushing off to the airport. I could read the whole book of Esther or the whole Gospel of Matthew, plus commentary notes. Or I could sing through all 150 Psalms. And after that I could meditate on what I'd read and pray about the concerns of my heart. I let God fill every hour of my day and every inch of my heart, and girl, it was *good!*

Often I spent time considering the discomfort I had endured after the complications occurred—the overwhelming pain, the time in the Intensive Care Unit, the blood transfusions, the hallucinations caused by the medications I was given (more about that in chapter 7). I thought about it all and wondered if I could ever be strong enough, courageous enough, to *choose* to go through that discomfort if it would spare someone I loved from enduring it. I thought of all that and how trivial my experience seemed compared with the prolonged agony Jesus *chose* to endure on my behalf: the humiliating trial, the brutal beating, the splintery weight of the cross on his bleeding shoulders as he dragged it toward Calvary, the crown of thorns piercing his brow, the nails pounded into his hands and feet.

I think of it and wonder, *Why, Lord? Why me? How could you go through so much to save a wretch like me?*

The answer rolls over me like a warm, soothing breeze on a cold day: *love.*

LEARNING FROM HEARTACHE

I learned so much during those long months of heartache! While the world of my usual activities swirled on without me, I grieved for the independence I had lost—but reveled in the enlightenment I gained during my housebound weeks. And now I tell you in all truth, that whole ordeal was one of the best things that ever happened to me.

Not that I would eagerly go through it all again! But I see now how much I learned during that time about my Savior and what he had done for me. I cherish the even deeper relationship with him that came about because of what happened to me. Adversity brought me closer to him.

The experience made me want to know how biblical women had survived broken hearts, and what they had learned from their experiences. Some of the most notable stories of heartache occurred because of a woman's deepest, unfulfilled longings. And frankly, some of them didn't seem to "get it," even when the lesson was obvious. Look at the story of Leah and Rachel, for instance, which is scattered over Genesis chapters 29 through 49. Both Leah and Rachel longed to have what the other already possessed.

Leah and Rachel were sisters married to the same man,

their cousin Jacob, who had actually wanted to marry only Rachel. But the girls' father, Laban, tricked Jacob into marrying Leah, the older sister, first. (If ever there were a lesson about partying too much on your wedding night, it's right there in Genesis 29:20–26. Jacob thought he had married Rachel, but when he woke up the next morning, he realized he'd unintentionally —and, we assume, drunkenly—consummated a marriage to Leah, whom his father-in-law had sneaked into his bed instead of Rachel.) Jacob eventually married Rachel too, and "he loved Rachel more than Leah" (v. 30).

What a heartache Leah must have endured, knowing her own father had tricked her sister's fiancé into marrying her—and knowing her husband would always love her sister more. In fact, the King James Version says, "Leah was hated" (v. 31). Imagine being trapped in such a situation *for the rest of your life*.

Leah's heartache is confirmed in the names she gave her first two sons: Affliction and Unloved. Uh-huh. That's what she named them: *Reuben*, which means "affliction," and *Simeon*, which means "unloved" (see Genesis 29:32–33). She conceived again, and when she delivered a third son she hoped her husband's attitude toward her would finally change. She named the son *Levi*, which means "attached."

By this point she had apparently given up on feeling loved but hoped a third son would at least make her husband feel a little more attached to her.

Finally we get a hint that Leah must have been sick and tired of feeling sick and tired; it must have occurred to her that her poor attitude was getting her nowhere. So when her fourth son was born, she named him *Judah*, which means "praise" (see Genesis 29:35).

Later, Leah had two more sons, for a total of six. Meanwhile, Jacob's other wife, the beloved Rachel, was barren.

So there they were, the two sisters, each with what the other wanted. Leah had given birth to four fine sons, but what she really wanted was to feel loved by her husband. Rachel was their husband's favorite; Jacob loved her so much he worked fourteen years for his father-in-law to pay Laban for the privilege of marrying Rachel. And yet Rachel wanted what Leah had: she wanted sons.

We have to believe things were a little tense in Jacob's household, judging by such passages as Genesis 30:1–2:

When Rachel saw that she was not bearing Jacob any children, she became jealous of her sister. So she said to Jacob, "Give me children, or I'll die!"

Jacob became angry with her and said, "Am I in the place of God, who has kept you from having children?"

After all these years, Rachel is still Jacob's favorite; he loves her intensely. But even in his love for her, he gets tired of her whining and complaining and acting like a victim. And right there we learn at least one important lesson that comes from studying this hornet's nest of a family: nobody wants to hear a nagging woman. Even a man who's consumed with love and affection for his wife can get sick of listening to the constant repetition of someone beset with a bad attitude. We've gotta zip it, girlfriend, or find something new and pleasant to say!

In desperation, Rachel gave her servant Bilhah to Jacob to "bear children for me" (Genesis 30:3). And sure enough, Bilhah delivered two sons to Jacob, prompting an apparently math-impaired Rachel to proclaim, "I have had a great struggle with my sister, and I have won" (v. 8). We almost get the idea at this point that the frustrated and jealous Rachel didn't so much want to become a mother as she wanted to compete with her big sister.

Not to be outdone, Leah gave her servant Zilpah to Jacob, resulting in two more sons. Then Leah had another child herself, a daughter.

So here are all these kids running around (Leah's seven plus Bilhah's and Zilpah's two each), and all these hormonal women—not only Leah and Rachel but also Bilhah and Zilpah (who couldn't have been all that thrilled that their sons had been claimed by two other women). And as if that wasn't enough of a challenge for Jacob to manage, about that time Rachel finally got pregnant. She gave birth to a boy and named him Joseph.

You might think she could finally be happy, finally feel contented. But was she? Judge for yourself. Scripture tells us the name *Joseph* means, "may the LORD add to me another son" (Genesis 30:22). One wasn't enough. She wanted another son, and God gave her one, a baby she named Ben-Oni, which means "son of my trouble."

Rachel died giving birth to him.

Look at this story and learn the lessons that come from a family created in deceit and continuously filled with jealousy and a lack of gratitude. Do you suppose there was one peaceful moment in this turbulent, emotion-filled household? Was this a happy home? Not a chance. The wives hated each other, and apparently they taught their sons to feel the same way.

God changed Jacob's name to Israel (and, by the way, Jacob had changed Rachel's son Ben-Oni's name to

Benjamin). I tell you this so it's easier to understand Genesis 37:3–4, which says, "Now Israel loved Joseph more than any of his other sons, because he had been born to him in his old age; and he made a richly ornamented robe for him. When his brothers saw that their father loved him more than any of them, they hated him and could not speak a kind word to him."

In fact, when Joseph was seventeen, his brothers decided to kill him! But the eldest, Reuben, talked them out of it; instead they sold him into slavery and told Jacob he'd been killed by a wild animal.

Here's another instance of that lesson we learned back in chapter 4 when we discussed the unlikelihood that God would use a Hebrew baby set adrift in the Nile to bring about a nation's release from captivity. God *will* use who and what he chooses to fulfill his will. Who would have thought he would choose a family as dysfunctional as Jacob's to create "a nation and a community of nations . . . , and kings will come from your body" (Genesis 35:11). It doesn't matter if it's unlikely. God doesn't care whether it makes sense to us. In fact, he seems to delight in using the unexpected, the least likely, or the weakest link to turn our lives upside down and inside out . . . and fulfill the plan he has had in mind since the beginning of time.

And here's another thing to consider: Jacob's family included umpteen children and at least four mothers. What fun they could have had, joking over the antics of all those wild-and-crazy boys, commiserating whose kids' clothes were dirtiest that week, gathering around the supper table in a joyful, lively scene that might have inspired Norman Rockwell to expand his holiday-dinner scene several millennia later (well, if they had a table, that is).

Instead, the women in the family were consumed with jealousy and hatred for each other—and as a result those same emotions filled their home. Which reminds me of Marilyn Meberg's adage: emotions don't have brains. And also of my very own corollary: hormones don't have good sense. Anytime we let out our emotions and our hormones control us, it's a given that we will mess it up.

The house of Jacob was one messed-up bunch. Leah had son after son, a blessing that would have been considered great wealth in those days, but she wasn't happy; she wanted Jacob's love. Rachel had Jacob's love but wanted children. Eventually Rachel got what she wanted—two sons—and then lost everything when she died in childbirth. Jacob buried her along the road as the family moved from one place to another.

We don't know if Jacob turned to Leah for solace after

Rachel died so that finally she may have gotten what she wanted—or if he withdrew from her and devoted himself to a life of grief. We know only that Leah also died before Jacob did, so she may not have had him to herself for long. We know this because Jacob directed his sons to bury him in the same cave where he had buried Leah (see Genesis 49:31).

Rachel and Leah thought they knew what was best for themselves. They thought they knew what they needed to make themselves happy. God apparently had other ideas. He gave them many blessings, but not the blessing each of them hoped for, at least not in the way each had pictured it.

ANOTHER WAY OF ASKING

Hannah was another woman who longed to be a mother. She was also a woman whose story we can learn from

Like Rachel, Hannah was married to a man, Elkanah, who had two wives. And like Rachel, Hanna was her husband's favorite, even though Hannah was childless and the other wife, Peninnah, had children. The story is told in 1 Samuel 1, which describes yet another unhappy household and labels Peninnah as Hannah's "rival" who "kept provoking her in order to irritate her" (v. 6).

Peninnah was apparently goading Hannah because she

was childless. "This went on year after year. Whenever Hannah went up to the house of the LORD, her rival provoked her till she wept and would not eat" (v. 7).

Hannah yearned for a child of her own, so much so that Elkanah became concerned for her well-being. "Her husband would say to her, 'Hannah, why are you weeping? Why don't you eat? Why are you downhearted? Don't I mean more to you than ten sons?'" (v. 8).

Like Rachel, Hannah prayed for a son. But unlike Rachel, she didn't ask for a child just for her own sense of fulfillment. During one of the family's yearly trips to the temple in Shiloh, Hannah prayed earnestly, "O LORD Almighty, if you will only look upon your servant's misery and remember me, and not forget your servant but give her a son, then I will give him to the LORD for all the days of his life" (v. 11).

Other writers have pointed out that Hannah wasn't making a deal with God. She wasn't bargaining with him (something most of us may be familiar with: "Dear Lord, if you'll only let me pass this test I'll never stay up late partying again"). I checked five different Bible versions, and all of them in 1 Samuel 1:11 say Hannah made a "vow."

Hers was no passing promise she would forget about later. She prayed so fervently that the temple priest, Eli, accused Hannah of being drunk.

She answered, "Not so, my lord, . . . I am a woman who is deeply troubled. . . . I was pouring out my soul to the LORD. Do not take your servant for a wicked woman; I have been praying here out of my great anguish and grief."

Eli acknowledged her sincerity and told her, "Go in peace, and may the God of Israel grant you what you have asked of him" (vv. 15–17).

And that's exactly what happened. Hannah left the temple with a new attitude, one of peaceful faith. She "ate something, and her face was no longer downcast" (v. 18). She and her family returned to their home, and within the next year she gave birth to a son, Samuel.

Now, here's the thing about Hannah that amazes me . . . and also touches my heart. She kept her vow to God—literally. She had said if she had a son she would "give him to the LORD for all the days of his life," and she didn't mean she would rear him to be a godly man. She meant she would deliver him to the temple and turn him over to the priest to raise so that he could grow up serving God *totally* all the days of his life.

The Bible says she kept him with her until he was weaned. I'm thinking she never let him out of her sight, knowing their time together would be short. In those days, women usually nursed their babies longer than modern mamas do, so Samuel might have been two or three years old when he was weaned.

Think how cute kids are at that stage. Innocent and full of life, enthralled by the simplest things and running to their mothers when they need comfort, protection, and love. Curling up in Mom's lap for cuddles, kisses, and naps.

That's probably the age Samuel was when Hannah took him to the temple and gave him up to God. The Living Bible says, "though he was still so small, they took him to the Tabernacle in Shiloh" (1 Samuel 1:23). When I think of her doing that, I think of those awful, awful news stories that tell of canceled adoptions forcing toddlers to be pried out of the arms of the adoptive parents who have reared them and returned to their birth parents. We can't know the details of what happened that day Hannah took Samuel to the temple and gave him to Eli, the priest. But when I imagine the scene I hear the heart-rending cries of a little boy echoing off the walls of the temple, his arms outstretched to his mother as she tearfully turns and walks away, going home without him.

Now, the Bible does *not* depict this scene as one of sorrow, and we know the Bible is true. In fact, the second chapter of 1 Samuel begins with Hannah's prayer of praise and adoration for God, thanking him for blessing her as he has done.

And yet . . .

Although the writer of the Old Testament book of 1 Samuel is unknown, we suspect it was a man, as most scholars were in those times. And knowing how *some* men tend to avoid emotional issues, I just have to wonder if there wasn't a little more to this story than what is recorded. I mean no disrespect. What *is* recorded is, of course, totally true. Hannah was overjoyed to have given birth to a son and delighted to give him back to the Lord. But as a woman, I read between the lines and have to wonder if there wasn't some grief mixed with Hannah's gladness.

For one thing, she had turned her beloved boy over to Eli, whose parenting skills had to be just a little suspect because 1 Samuel 2:12, 17 says, "The sons of Eli were evil men who didn't love the Lord. . . . The sin of these young men was very great in the eyes of the Lord" (TLB).

Oh, dear! Could Eli protect little Samuel from these evil adult sons who preyed on worshipers bringing sacrifices to the temple?

And maybe there were little things too that brought secret tears to Hannah's heart. Would Eli remember Samuel needed his favorite blankie at bedtime? Would he sing to him the way Hannah had done? Would Eli know that little

Samuel liked crackers crumbled in his soup, not served on the side? Would he sit beside Samuel's bed when the boy was frightened at night or wipe his brow with a cool cloth when he had a fever?

Maybe I'm being silly. But I'm also a woman who has mothered three children and tended a passel of grandchildren. Just the thought of handing one of them over to someone else—forever—brings tears to my eyes. I could not do it without the kind of superhuman strength and resolve that comes from God alone. Surely Hannah felt the same way; surely she knew God would give her the miraculous fortitude she needed to fulfill her vow to him and survive the heartache.

Let's learn from Hannah. Let's incorporate her courage and faith into our lives today so that it's a continual, empowering presence in our hearts. When we face impossible losses and overwhelming sacrifices, let's believe without a doubt that our all-powerful God will get us through the difficulties. Let's know, as Hannah knew, that our God will give us the fortitude we need, and let's praise his holy name no matter what circumstances befall us.

That means when illness steals our health or setbacks take our wealth or disability replaces our independence, we cling to the God who helped Hannah give up the child

who was most precious to her. We know what she knew—
that he will see us through the hard times.

That means when we have to say to a loved one "good-
bye for now," as Kathy Troccoli sings so beautifully, we will
not collapse into a helpless heap of sorrow. We will grieve,
yes, but not as those who have no hope (see 1 Thessalonians
4:13). As believers blessed with the gift of salvation, we
know God will reunite us with those loved ones someday in
a place where there will be no more tears.

Thinking of Hannah, I remember also those parents,
spouses, and children whose loved ones are serving far
away in dangerous places right now. Those believers also
can empathize with Hannah and learn from her courage
and her faith; they too can proclaim, "For all the earth is
the Lord's and he has set the world in order. He will protect his godly ones" (1 Samuel 2:8–9 TLB). One way or
another, God *will* restore us to those dear ones.

ONCE BROKEN, NOW BETTER THAN EVER

I've told you how my spiritual life improved as my health
deteriorated. In my infirmity, I became closer to Jesus; in
severe pain, I appreciated even more the agony he willingly endured for me. Amazing goodness *can* come from

bewildering problems, impossible challenges, and broken hearts.

Leah and Rachel endured heartache, hatred, and upheaval, and their sons carried those problems into their own adulthood. Yet one of the most profound lessons of Scripture would come from that family's tremendous problems. When his brothers sold him into slavery, Joseph—the long-awaited son of Rachel and the favorite son of Jacob—ended up in Egypt, where, after surviving his own set of difficulties and challenges, he became a trusted official in Pharaoh's government.

Later, when famine destroyed all the crops in his original family's homeland, Joseph's brothers were forced to seek relief from—guess who!—that very official in Egypt. They did not recognize Joseph, but he knew immediately who they were. Granted, he made them jump through all sorts of hoops and endure headaches before he finally helped them. But eventually he told them who he was, and when they cowered in fear that he would wreak justice upon them, he instead extended grace, telling them, "You meant evil against me; but God meant it for good" (Genesis 50:20 NKJV).

Think of all the broken hearts in this story and how God used what seemed to be impossible situations to bring about amazing miracles. Jacob's twelve sons became the twelve tribes of Israel, some of whom are still warring today in the Middle East. When I get disheartened, thinking the situation there is also impossible, I remember how God has used other impossible situations to work his will, and I resolve to strengthen my hope and my faith.

And think of Hannah, who we suspect was brokenhearted to give up her precious son, Samuel. From her sacrifice came a great prophet who would anoint unlikely and unsuspecting kings-to-be and who would later even reproach those kings when they strayed from godly pathways. Samuel served God devotedly and selflessly. Something wonderful came from Hannah's barrenness . . . and, later, from what I privately suspect was a broken heart soothed by the joy of knowing she was walking in God's perfect path for her life. (And by the way, we're told Hannah and Elkanah had other children after Samuel.)

When hardships hit, when our heart breaks, of course we grieve for what we've lost. But in our sadness, let's resolve to learn through our grief. Let's ask God what he's trying to show us, what he's trying to teach us, through the difficult experience. That's a very familiar place for me to be, that place of questioning God. In fact I wrote a whole book about it, titled, *What's Going on, Lord?*

Sometimes the answer is immediately clear. Sometimes we may not realize until weeks or even years later what God was teaching us in our time of trial. We may not know until we get to heaven and can ask God face to face. Meanwhile, whether or not the specific lesson is immediately discernible, we need to let our heartache send us into God's loving embrace, knowing what the girls of the Bible—and my sweet old Granny—now know too: God *will* make a way.

⚜ 6 ⚜

Bad Apples, Hard Hearts, and Strong Lessons

If you set your heart on God
and reach out to him,
If you scrub your hands of sin
and refuse to entertain evil in your home,
You'll be able to face the world unashamed
and keep a firm grip on life, guiltless and
fearless.

—Job 11:13–15 MSG

I WAS IN A HEAVENLY SHOPPING MALL—MY KIND of place! There was this great, big, beautiful, snow-white Christmas tree with one satiny, white ornament—just gorgeous. "Oh!" I said to my daughter. "Can you see that? It's beautiful."

Beyond the tree I spotted some very interesting LL Bean bags.

My family told me later that I said, "Do you see those white LL Bean bags? Y'all need to go buy some of those bags."

That's when they knew I was hallucinating. I've never bought anything from LL Bean, never looked in a catalog, never thought about needing any LL Bean gear as long as I've lived.

Then everything changed. Suddenly, I was running faster than I've ever run—running for my life, dodging and jumping over heinous, evil forces that were trying to grab me. The pink bunnies were the worst, but the pink cap pistols and pink peanut patties were almost as bad. "They're going to kill me," I yelled to my husband. "I know they're going to kill me." Then I added matter-of-factly, "Yeah, they're killing me."

Modern medication can do amazing things: ward off infections, promote healing, ease pain. But it can also send us into silly—or horrifying—hallucinations. Sometimes both. And of course the terror-filled dreams are the worst. It doesn't matter that the nightmares are outlandish and silly when described later. When they play out in *your* head, they can be serious and overwhelming.

I was sedated a long time during my second hospitalization and second surgery, and sometime early in that week, I was given a medication that sent me on a trip to the netherworld. It gave me a quick glimpse of fun and then a tiny glimpse of hell—but enough for me to know I never want to see it again. I'm happy to turn it over completely to the unbelievers!

Yes, the villains in my hallucination were ridiculously cute, but that did not decrease my terror. Those pink rabbits, pink cap pistols, and pink peanut patties were as murderously vicious as the most violent horror-movie monsters. I guess it was quite a scene when I tried to jump straight up from my hospital bed to escape. My husband said later I was trying so frantically to get out of that bed that the nurse gave me more medication, which apparently canceled out whatever had caused the bad trip, and I gradually returned to reality.

But the memory of the dream—and my remembered terror—still remain. At first it was frustrating to share the dream with my family members—and have them laugh at me. I couldn't believe I was telling them about something that had tried to kill me, and they were laughing. Wouldn't *you* be upset? OK, so it was a pink peanut patty. But didn't they get it? I had nearly died a horrible death! Or, at least, I had dreamed I nearly died. And they were laughing!

The terror I felt—and remembered—made a bad situation even worse. I was already in great misery. Experiencing a night terror on top of everything else that was happening to me seemed like way more than I should be expected to handle. And yet, as often happens when God makes a way, something good came of even that hallucination.

I certainly don't condone violence or criminal behavior of any kind, but now I have a greater understanding of how it is committed by those who use illicit, hallucinatory drugs. I can understand now how such substances send drug users out of their minds. Before I lived through my own hallucinations, I had no idea what a strong psychotic influence drugs can have on a person. But remembering the terror that consumed me during my own drug-induced trip, I know that, had I been able to get out of that bed, somebody might have gotten hurt as I tried to flee the imaginary demons. I was in torment, and anyone who had tried to physically stop me from escaping that terror would have been in danger.

Even as I write these words, I realize it's probably as hard for you to imagine being physically afraid of a short, sick, silver-haired great-grandmother on a tirade as it is to imagine yourself ever thinking that pink bunnies and pink peanut patties would try to kill you. That's why I say you really have to experience it yourself to understand how it can happen.

Maybe it would be easier for you to accept the other thing my family reported about my behavior while I was on those drugs. My son-in-law told me, "Mama T, you talked and talked and talked, and you prayed and prayed and prayed— apparently for everybody on the planet. And when you got all through prayin', you said, 'And God, I know you can do anything—you can even heal bootie rash.'"

All right, now, maybe it's time to move on. I've opened this chapter with a description of my wild experience in dreamland to help you start thinking about things that are different than they seem. In this chapter we're going to look at some women who might look like ordinary characters at first glance but who, like the pink bunnies in my nightmare, are actually something else entirely. Some of these women might have been thought of as bad girls during their time but are admired and respected now. Others were bad to the bone—but their stories have redeeming value today. Either way, these are women we can learn from, positively or negatively, when we study what they knew and what they did.

A HARLOT HEROINE

Let's start with a couple of women whose sexual virtue was questionable. One of them, Rahab, is clearly labeled a prostitute in Joshua 2:1; she was a bad apple in the eyes of her society. But even though she was guilty of sexual misconduct, her story provides us with very important lessons thousands of years later.

Rahab's name first appears when Joshua had taken over from Moses the responsibility of leading the people of Israel into the Promised Land. He sent two spies ahead to check out the land, specifically the city of Jericho.

Now, here's one of those little glitches in the story that still puzzles me. Joshua tells these two men to go spy out the land, and the very next sentence in Joshua 2:1 has them staying "at the house of a harlot named Rahab." You get the feeling they got a weekend pass to head into town, and the first thing they did was head for a house of prostitution! And the Bible clearly says they "*stayed* there." We'd like to think they sneaked around the city and did a little work to gather information and carry out their mission, but *noooooooo*. They just hung out with Rahab.

Now, some scholars say that Rahab was an innkeeper, and that's why the two men showed up there. Maybe so, but I'm still not impressed by these two guys. The *next* verses say the king of Jericho found out about them and sent word to Rahab to "bring out the men who came to you to stay the night in your house" (v. 3 MSG). So that, too, makes me wonder: just how good at spying could they be if, at the first place they stop, they're detected and called out by the king? There's a part of me that thinks Rahab became a heroine of our faith simply because she took pity on a couple of unintelligent intelligence agents!

We don't know for sure what her impression of the two spies was. We only know what she thought of their God. Here's what she told the men:

> I know that GOD has given you the land. We're all afraid. Everyone in the country feels hopeless. We heard how GOD dried up the waters of the Red Sea before you when you left Egypt, and what he did to the two Amorite kings east of the Jordan, Sihon and Og, whom you put under a holy curse and destroyed. We heard it and our hearts sank. We all had the wind knocked out of us. And all because of you, you and GOD, your God, God of the heavens above and God of the earth below. (Joshua 2:9–11 MSG)

Rahab had heard about the Israelites' God, and she believed what she heard—so strongly that she risked her own life to protect the two spies. She didn't turn them over to the king; she lied to his messengers and said they had already left. She hid them until it was safe for them to leave, then she lowered them down out of her window, which was on the outer edge of the city wall. The spies went back to Joshua and reported what Rahab had said about the residents' fear of the Israelites and their God, and it wasn't long before the walls of Jericho fell. But Rahab and her relatives were spared.

Rahab teaches us the truth of that old adage about not judging a book by its cover. Rahab was a harlot. She might have been an innkeeper too, as others suggest. But there is no doubt about her life as a prostitute. That's how she's described in all six Bible translations I checked. We can only imagine what her fellow citizens of Jericho thought of her. Probably the same things we tend to think about prostitutes today! They're criminals (in most states), immoral and virtueless.

But maybe we need to reexamine our attitudes, our judgment, about prostitutes—and all those today who are identified by unflattering labels. Maybe we need to look at them through God's eyes and see their potential rather than their present situation. That's clearly how God viewed Rahab; we know he recognized her potential because through her—a heathen harlot—would come the lineage of the Messiah, God's own Son (see Matthew 1:5). You'd better believe he saw great potential in her!

Is there someone out there in your circle of contacts—the beggar at that intersection you drive through every day, the never-married mother of a houseful of children down the street, the pierced and tattooed kid who works at your neighborhood video store—that you have automatically labeled instead of looking at through God's eyes? I'm not saying you have to invite these people to your house for supper, but I *am* suggesting that we all take care to maintain a godly attitude toward everyone and view even the strangest among us with a God's-eyes perspective. We are to pray for them and think of them with the same love God shows us.

And I don't know about you, girlfriend, but sometimes—like when I'm laid up in a hospital bed with a hinged, metal plate stapled to my stomach and terrifying pink bunnies and pink peanut patties causing me to jump and holler like a crazy woman—I ain't much to look at!

A KING'S MISTRESS

Now let's look at another woman, Bathsheba, who was also involved in sexual misconduct, although her part in the affair was more mysterious than Rahab's. We don't know if Bathsheba was the innocent victim of a peeping-Tom king or a conniving floosie who deliberately enticed him to seduce her. What we do know is that King David (Rahab's great-great grandson; see Matthew 1:5–6) acted inappropriately in giving in to his lust for Bathsheba. And in the story of what happened next, we can learn from what the two of them learned.

Bathsheba was a beautiful woman whose husband was away at war, fighting on behalf of King David. We don't know why the king wasn't out there fighting the enemy too, but he wasn't. He was at home in the palace with his many wives and concubines. One night when he was looking out over the city, he spotted, on a nearby rooftop, a beautiful woman, bathing. And that's where all the questions begin: 2 Samuel 11: 2 says David was strolling along his own roof because he couldn't sleep. So it must have been full dark—and yet he could see a woman bathing on another rooftop. Had Bathsheba lit a torch so she could be seen by anyone who happened to be looking?

And just how—and what—was she bathing? Was she completely naked, or was she just soaking her feet? Verse 4 says Bathsheba "had just completed the purification rites after menstruation" (TLB), which opens up another category of bathing possibilities. The truth is, we don't know why or what Bathsheba was bathing on her roof late that night. But we know King David saw her and sent for her.

We assume she had no choice but to heed the king's summons. But what happened next opens up yet another group of questions. Verse 4 also says David "slept with her. . . . Then she went back home." Other Bible versions say "he lay with her." Interestingly, none of the translations I checked say he raped her.

So if it wasn't rape, was it consensual? Was she, indeed, a bad apple? Was this the sensuous result of a scheme she'd been cooking up for a long time? Or did she give in to the king's command, believing she had no choice? We don't know. But we do know that later, when David got Bathsheba's message saying she was pregnant, he concocted a scheme of his own to get her husband, Uriah, home from the battlefield.

David hoped Uriah would "sleep" with Bathsheba and thus believe the child was his. But the loyal Uriah was so devoted to his king and his fellow soldiers he refused to go home to his wife and instead slept at the palace entryway, guarding his respected sovereign.

If we list crimes worse than adultery, murder surely goes at the top of the list. And David committed both those immoral deeds. He ordered Uriah moved to the front lines, where he would most certainly be killed. When the inevitable happened, David married Bathsheba and eagerly awaited the birth of their child.

There is so much about this story we don't know. Yet we can assume that, even though David had other wives and concubines, and even though he may have impregnated other women in his harem—or in his kingdom—without falling head over heels in love with them, Bathsheba was different. David was totally smitten, completely consumed, in his desire (and we assume, love) for her—so much so that he had her husband killed so he could marry her himself.

Not surprisingly, "the thing David had done displeased the LORD" (2 Samuel 11:26), and God "struck the child that Uriah's wife had borne to David, and he became ill" (2 Samuel 12:15). Despite David's pleas, prayers, and fasting, the baby boy died when he was a week old.

We know that the relationship of parents who experience the death of a child can either be strengthened or weakened as they endure such a devastating loss. When the child's death is directly attributed to the action of one of the parents (in this case, David's causing Bathsheba's lawful husband to be killed in battle), we have to think the strain on that relationship is especially difficult.

Yet despite this challenge, David and Bathsheba's marriage seemed to grow. David humbled himself before

God, begged for forgiveness, and renewed his devotion to God—and lucky for us he did! Because his and Bathsheba's next child, Solomon, was granted the gift of wisdom by God, and through him the Messiah was descended (see Matthew 1:6–7).

And here we are, back at the corner of Unlikely and Farfetched, amazed at the misfits and wrongdoers God chose for his Son's ancestors. Unless you know the wonderful way God delights in using the least likely to do the most marvelous, you wouldn't expect to find someone who committed both adultery and murder in Jesus's lineage. But there's old David, named in Matthew 1:6 along with "the widow of Uriah" (TLB). And we're shown again that, except for blatantly cursing the Holy Spirit, you can't do anything that will make God cast you out.

LEARNING FROM BATHSHEBA

We might be a little suspicious of Bathsheba's character in the beginning of this story, but the more we study her, the more we see her wisdom and her strong love for God. Many scholars believe she was the mother of Lemuel, as well as Solomon. Thus she is thought to be the original source of the inspiring description and instructional advice in Proverbs 31, which begins with, "The sayings of King Lemuel—an oracle his mother taught him."

When you consider that Bathsheba may have passed down the advice in Proverbs 31, you can't help but detect some sharp irony. If, indeed, she was the source for this wisdom, we have to believe that she was passing on knowledge she learned the hard way through her own tragic experience. In light of that possibility, consider what might have been going through her mind as she wrote such statements as these:

Who can find a virtuous and capable wife?
    She is more precious than rubies.
Her husband can trust her,
    and she will greatly enrich his life.
She brings him good, not harm,
    all the days of her life. (vv. 10–12)

Her children stand and bless her.
    Her husband praises her:
"There are many virtuous and capable women in the world,
    but you surpass them all!"
Charm is deceptive, and beauty does not last;
    but a woman who fears the LORD will be greatly praised.

Reward her for all she has done.

Let her deeds publicly declare her praise. (vv. 28–31 NLT)

When you read Proverbs 31 thinking Bathsheba may have written it, you see it in a whole different light, don't you? This girl knew a lot about life and a lot about marriage. And one way or another, she had learned a lot about virtue!

Ain't God somethin'? He took a scandal and, several generations later, used it to give the world the One who would bring us salvation. What a tremendous act of forgiveness, mercy, and grace.

When I think of David and Bathsheba, I remember a story shared by my friend Lynda Wigren (Barbara Johnson's sidekick whose big heart and crazy antics are shared in many of Barb's books). Lynda had recently read a book comparing justice, mercy, and grace, and she said it led her to feel God gripping her heart to reveal little opportunities for her to live out what she had learned.

For example, Lynda's father lives with her and her husband, and when his hearing aid broke, she took it to the repair shop, which promised to have it ready by Wednesday, but it wasn't. Thursday it still wasn't fixed, but the repair guy promised it would be ready Friday. When Lynda went back on Friday, the shop was closed. She returned on Saturday, and it was still closed. On Monday she called and was told the hearing aid wasn't fixed yet.

If Lynda had practiced *justice*, she might have yelled at the repair guy, told him how incompetent and undependable he was, then angrily retrieved the hearing aid and vowed never to do business with him again. By practicing *mercy*, she told him, "That's OK. I understand. We all get behind sometimes." But Lynda went beyond that. She practiced *grace*. She went out and bought the harried repair guy a box of candy and dropped it off as a little gift of encouragement. Can you imagine the impression her gracious act made on this overworked man? Especially when you compare it to what might have happened to him if Thelma Wells had been there and, without God's miraculous intervention, suffered one of her infamous meltdown tirades? Oh, girl, instead of seeing God's goodness in one of his earthly servants, he might have witnessed a spectacular demonstration of humanity's depravity!

God responded to the adulterous relationship of David and Bathsheba with justice (the heartbreaking death of their child) but also with extravagant grace. He washed away their sin in a tidal wave of love and blessed them with more children, one of whom would carry on the lineage of the Messiah.

Now I ask you again: ain't God somethin'? All of us need to experience his glorious goodness, the kind received by David and Bathsheba—the kind spelled out in Romans 5:20–21:

> But sin didn't, and doesn't, have a chance in competition with the aggressive forgiveness we call grace. When it's sin versus grace, grace wins hands down. All sin can do is threaten us with death, and that's the end of it. Grace, because God is putting everything together again through the Messiah, invites us into life—a life that goes on and on and on, world without end. (MSG)

We see so much in the knowledge Bathsheba gained through her experience. She knew what it was like to grieve. She knew how deeply we can be scarred by sin. But she also knew what it was like to receive God's amazing grace and mercy. Undoubtedly she learned it— or relearned it—along with her husband David, the source of Psalm 51:1:

> *[For the director of music. A psalm of David. When the prophet Nathan came to him after David had committed adultery with Bathsheba.]* Have mercy on me, O God, according to your

unfailing love; according to your great compassion blot out my transgressions.

I encourage you to read the rest of Psalm 51. Feel the sorrow and guilt David was expressing, and then marvel at the way God answered his (and, no doubt, Bathsheba's) prayer: "Purify me from my sins, and I will be clean; wash me, and I will be whiter than snow. Oh, give me back my joy again;   you have broken me—now let me rejoice" (vv. 7–8 NLT).

And finally, let me remind you: what God did for David and Bathsheba, he can do for you too.

THE QUEEN OF TERROR

Now, before we close this chapter about bad apples and hard hearts, I want to mention the baddest bad apple of all time: Jezebel. Somehow this heathen nightmare of a woman became queen of Israel, where she wreaked terror and death on her people. My Bible's commentary says, "She committed many atrocious crimes to those who were faithful and obedient to God."

Jezebel and her husband, King Ahab, were quite a pair. Here's a glimpse into their reputation:

Ahab son of Omri did more evil in the eyes of the LORD than any of those before him. He not only considered it trivial to commit the sins of Jeroboam son of Nebat, but he also married Jezebel . . . , and began to serve Baal and worship him. . . . Ahab also made an Asherah pole and did more to provoke the LORD, the God of Israel, to anger than did all the kings of Israel before him. . . .

There was never a man like Ahab, who sold himself to do evil in the eyes of the LORD, urged on by Jezebel his wife. (1 Kings 16:30–31, 33; 21:25)

Oh, wouldn't you just love to have this couple leading your country?

Ahab and Jezebel's reign was truly a time of terror for the people of Israel, and judging by the verses above, we suspect that Jezebel pressured her husband to commit the evil and immoral deeds he unleashed upon his people.

Reading their story in the books of 1 and 2 Kings, we see the harmful characteristics of this evil woman—and we learn strong lessons from her wicked ways. She led her husband astray right from the beginning, converting him from his God-fearing faith to worship of the heathen god Baal. Oh, sisters, let's be careful never to lead our loved ones away from the almighty and all-powerful God! Let's make sure we steer completely clear of any remotely evil influences that our family members might see us reading or watching or listening to, causing them to mistakenly assume we endorse that kind of wickedness.

Let's make sure we don't fall for the enticements of idols. While Baal may not be a common threat in today's world of believers, there are still plenty of idols out there to distract us—idols such as money, possessions, status, or other things that plant in us the little seeds of discontent and discord that we may pass on—intentionally or unintentionally—to others.

Let's be a positive force in our husbands' lives. Let's encourage them to exude goodness and mercy toward all those around them. And, seeing Jezebel's evil ways, let's be especially careful not to take on a controlling spirit—both at home and wherever we go. It's easy to spot Jezebel's controlling spirit in many people today. I see it in families, where one spouse or one adult child tries to control the action and thought of every other family member.

And, perhaps saddest of all, I've seen it in churches, where control-hungry members use money or gifts or attention to pressure the pastor into preaching the way *they* want him to preach, to lead the church in the direction *they* have in mind.

I've seen the Jezebel spirit in organizations where participants continually offer "constructive criticism" to undermine the leadership and plant disruptive elements of discord.

GIVING UP CONTROL

Girlfriend, I have to confess to you that I have had a Jezebel spirit at times during my life. I've wanted to control my husband, my children, my home, my environment, and everything around me. And honestly, there have been times when I've given it my best shot, trying to make everything work, and all I've done is make everyone miserable.

Uh-huh. That's right. Sweet little 'ol Mama T has tried to rule the world—or at least my own rambunctious family and ministries—and the results have been disastrous. You may not be *quite* as surprised to learn that fact as I was when it was revealed to me through some very powerful and beneficial counseling.

I was going through some agonizing upheavals in my life that had produced in me very un-Thelma-like feelings of depression, bitterness, and vengeance—even thoughts of violence! Girl, on a scale of 0–10, my anger back then was a 15! I was *consumed* with these unfamiliar (and, in my mind, completely justified) emotions. And I knew I needed help in handling them, before I actually hurt someone.

I sought out certified Christian counselors who helped me sort through my problems as well as my feelings about them. They joined me in fervent prayer asking God to help me with these feelings and tell him, "I don't want this! I don't want to feel this way anymore. What do you want me to do, Lord?"

In my heart I felt God telling me, "Thelma, you are a controller."

Well, as if to confirm that he was totally correct, I argued with him! I'm a type A personality, and I said, "Oh no, God. You have me mixed up with someone else. You don't make mistakes. I know that. However—how-*ev*-uh—you are wrong this time, Lord. You have miscalled it."

If that's not being a controller (or trying to be), I don't know what is!

God repeated the statement again . . . and then again: "Thelma, you are a controller."

I started bawling. I cried, and I cried, and I cried, and I cried, thinking of the wicked, conniving, controlling Jezebel and begging God to please, please, *please* remove from me anything that could be even slightly similar to her evil spirit. None of us wants to see ourselves negatively, but through that counseling process, I saw a *big* nodule of negativity in my life, and I asked God to help me eliminate it.

And, praise Jesus, he did. He helped me see that—what a surprise—I'm not in control of anything. He is.

He controls everything and everyone, and if I have a problem with that, I've learned to take it up with *him* before I spout off to the person involved. People who need to change are only going to change if they perceive that a benefit will come to them if they do. That's what I learned. And the benefit I reap by giving up my attempts at control is a great sense of peace and comforting faith, knowing God will make a way through whatever the disturbing issue is.

It took me a long, long time, but I finally learned—for real—what Granny taught me all those years ago. In the meantime, I lived out too often those cherished words from the old, beloved hymn:

> Oh, what peace we often forfeit,
> Oh, what needless pain we bear,
> All because we do not carry
> Everything to God in prayer.

I am much less argumentative now than I used to be. When something or someone upsets me, I talk to God before

I talk to the other person. I still speak up when that's what's needed, but I ask God first, "How should I deal with this, Father?" And sometimes I feel him directing me to be still and keep quiet as he melts the Jezebel spirit out of me.

Jezebel paid for her evil, in part, by dying a gruesome death. She was thrown out a window, trampled by horses, and then eaten by dogs (see 2 Kings 9:30–37). We assume she's now condemned to eternally swimming laps in the devil's lake of fire (see Revelation 20:14), but we can't know for sure—and I certainly don't intend to check in there to find out!

Learning from Those Who Learned the Hard Way

By studying the lives of Rahab, Bathsheba, and Jezebel, we learn how God can use bad apples (or, in the case of Bathsheba, perhaps only "blemished" fruit) to teach us lessons today. Rahab, a harlot, was surely among the lowest of the low in her society. Yet she listened and learned about the Israelites' God, and she followed her heart to believe what she heard. As a result she was moved to help God's people, and in doing so she saved herself and her family, not just from the destruction of war but for all eternity. Her bold actions led her to become part of the family of Jesus—both in this world and the next.

Bathsheba's story invites us to consider the mysteries of her heart. We cannot know whether she was a willing accomplice in a treacherous conspiracy of adultery, or whether everything that occurred happened against her will. We can safely assume, however, that once the adultery occurred, especially when she became pregnant while her husband was away at war, she would have been shamed and ridiculed by her community.

She suffered tremendous losses, the deaths of her husband and her infant son. And yet, like Rahab, she overcame her trials to join the Messiah's earthly and eternal family.

From Jezebel we learn that disobedience to God's plan for us may begin in our hearts and minds. Whenever we give in to temptations to do bad instead of good, whenever we yield to misguided urges to snatch control from God and go our own way, we can easily end up causing immeasurable harm, not only for ourselves but for others too. Oh, Lord, spare us all from the kind of evil Jezebel demonstrated! Take the Jezebel spirit out of us and replace it with your spirit of loving and gracious subservience.

Each morning I ask God to equip me to withstand "the wiles of the devil" that may come at me that day

(Ephesians 6:11 KJV). I know Satan is out there, lying in wait and hoping to lure me off the godly pathway. Our modern world is packed full of momentary troubles and appealing temptations that can end up being deadly diversions for our souls. Studying Scripture helps us learn to discern God's way from the world's way. Prayer enables us to endure those situations that might lead us astray. And faith helps us know that God is in control.

❧ 7 ❧

Nobodies Who Got Noticed: From Something Little, God Makes Much

God sees not as man sees, for man looks at the outward appearance, but the LORD looks at the heart.

—*1 Samuel 16:7 NASB*

LAST YEAR THE HOUSING AUTHORITY OF DALLAS published a commemorative calendar featuring photos of successful people who had lived in the projects. And what do you know? There's Thelma Wells, Miss May 2006.

The calendar, published annually, is intended to encourage those who come from homes that aren't ever gonna show up on *Livestyles of the Rich and Famous*, and I was happy to be identified as one of many successful role models who came from a public-housing background. My younger years were spent in my great-grandparents' back-alley apartment, but when Daddy Harrell died, Granny's financial situation meant she could no longer afford the apartment rent. So off we went to Roseland Homes.

Now, before you go feelin' sorry for me, let me quote from my page on the Housing Authority calendar:

> In the 1940's and 50's, the projects were looked upon as a safe and clean place to live. . . . We were a watching community with everyone's interest at heart. . . .
>
> Living in a community of friends and people who were Christians, for the most part, created a caring atmosphere of safety and high moral values.

Not that I'm the greatest thing since air conditioning, but I've done OK for someone who grew up where I did. And not that my work could ever compare with some of the hardworking believers out there whose ministries have impacted tens of millions of people, but I've done what I can. In my own small way, I've carried the gospel to my own neighborhood as well as to foreign countries, and through Women of Faith and my own two organizations, A Woman of God Ministries and the Daughters of Zion Mentoring Program, I've done my best to extend God's loving kindness toward my fellow human beings. Wherever I go, I wear my bumblebee pin and assure others that in Christ they can BEE their best.

I hope others see me as someone who overcame challenges and adversities to achieve success—and that my experience gives them confidence and encouragement to do the same, no matter what their circumstances are. That desire prompts me, in this final chapter, to point out to you some of the little-known biblical women who've inspired and encouraged me along the way. They aren't as "famous" as Eve, or Jesus's mother Mary, or Mary Magdalene, and they didn't get whole Bible books named after them, as Esther and Ruth did. Some of them aren't even named. But by studying their stories, we discern what they knew and how that knowledge led them to do something—maybe something big or small, maybe something humble or daring, maybe even some wayward action—that was noted and remembered. What they did might have seemed insignificant at the time. But here we are, thousands of years later, still learning from them.

THE NOBODIES HALL OF FAME

Biblical times were strongly patriarchal. No question about it: men ruled the roost. So for a woman even to be mentioned in the Bible we have to assume that what she did was really memorable. Interestingly, the apostle Paul, who is cited most often by some denominations as restraining women from taking leadership roles (see 1 Timothy 2), is also the New Testament writer who frequently commended women for their work in spreading the gospel.

For example, Phoebe is the first name mentioned when Paul starts his list of acknowledgments in Romans 16, and just look how glowingly he introduces her:

> I commend to you our sister Phoebe, who is a deacon in the church in Cenchrea. Welcome her in the Lord as one who is worthy of honor among God's people. Help her in whatever she needs, for she has been helpful to many, and especially to me. (vv. 1–2, NLT)

This is the only time she's mentioned, but those few sentences say a lot, don't they? Wouldn't you love to share a cup of coffee with Phoebe today and ask her about her work in the early church, a time when Christians were persecuted and maligned? Wouldn't you love to know exactly how she was "helpful to many" and especially to Paul?

We can't know exactly what she did. But from Paul's words we know what she knew: that Jesus is the Messiah. And that knowledge empowered her to become an inspiring, dedicated, courageous worker for the gospel.

In Romans 16, Paul also commended Aquila and his wife, Priscilla (we'll discuss them a little later in this chapter). And he mentioned "Andronicus and Junias, my relatives who have been in prison with me. They are outstanding among the apostles, and they were in Christ before I was" (v. 7). Many scholars believe *Junias* was actually *Junia* (the name used in the King James Version), and that Junia was a woman. You can imagine the controversy this creates, since Paul calls her an apostle. I'll leave the arguing for others, but I can't help but enjoy just considering the possibility.

I'm also intrigued by the short, simple, five-word reference to Philip the evangelist's "four unmarried daughters who prophesied" (Acts 21:9). In those few words we see the passing of the torch, a second generation taking up the cause of Christ and carrying it forward. Oh, if only their words and work had been recorded! Again, we don't know exactly what they said and did, but we are inspired by what we know they *knew*—and how they acted upon it.

A similar passing of the torch is shown in Paul's second letter to his coworker Timothy. As he begins the letter, he encourages Timothy to do powerful work by first reminding him of his heritage:

> I have been reminded of your sincere faith, which first lived in your grandmother Lois and in your mother Eunice and, I am persuaded, now lives in you also. For this reason I remind you to fan into flame the gift of God, which is in you through the laying on of my hands. For God did not give us a spirit of timidity, but a spirit of power, of love and of self-discipline. (2 Timothy 1:5–7)

Only this once are these two women, Timothy's mother and grandmother, mentioned in the Bible. But that brief reference creates in our minds an image we want to duplicate. We picture Timothy watching his mother and grandmother, being inspired by the way they lived their lives, and learning from what they knew. And that image inspires us to let our own children and grandchildren see us live godly lives and bring them along as we move ever closer to the Savior.

A servant girl (talk about a nobody!) named Rhoda is mentioned in a little spot of comedy in Acts 12:11–17. The church had been earnestly praying for the apostle Peter, who had been imprisoned by King Herod. The night before he was to go on trial, Peter was miraculously released from prison by an angel of the Lord. At first, Peter couldn't believe what was happening; he thought he was having a vision. When he finally "came to himself" (v. 11), he went to the home of Mary, mother of John (also called Mark), where "many people had gathered and were praying" (v. 12).

And that's when we get our laugh. Here's how the story is told in Acts 12:13–16:

> Peter knocked at the outer entrance, and a servant girl named Rhoda came to answer the door. When she recognized Peter's voice, she was so overjoyed she ran back without opening it and exclaimed, "Peter is at the door!"
>
> "You're out of your mind," they told her. When she kept insisting that it was so, they said, "It must be his angel."
>
> But Peter kept on knocking, and when they opened the door and saw him, they were astonished.

Poor Rhoda! I'm sure she *meant* to open the door. But in her joyful excitement, and in her eagerness to share the good news that Peter was out of prison, she evidently slammed the door in Peter's face and left him standing on the doorstep as she rushed off to tell the others he was there.

Reading this sweet little story, I marvel that such a funny anecdote made its way into Scripture. But we know its inclusion is no accident. There's no mindless "filler" in God's Word! So I've enjoyed pondering what wisdom can be gained by studying Rhoda the servant girl.

Could it be that her story reminds us to "walk the walk" as well as "talk the talk"? Rhoda was full of talk; she couldn't wait to tell the others Peter had come to them. But she didn't act. She didn't open that door! How many of us are "big talkers," pouring out words in enthusiastic praise and prayer, but not taking action? We don't invite Jesus into our hearts. We don't make him our closest Friend, our personal Savior. We don't really follow a Christlike path. Sure, we *sound* good. But do we *live* as good as we sound?

Let's look at one more nobody before we move on. Unlike Rhoda, Tabitha (also known as Dorcas), wasn't remembered in Scripture necessarily for her words. She was remembered for her kindness—and for what happened to her because of her many friends' devotion to her. Acts 9:36 says she was a disciple who was "always doing good and helping the poor." One good thing she evidently did was make clothes for others. We assume this because, when she died, her friends summoned the apostle Peter to the room where they had laid out her body, and they showed him the "robes and other clothing that Dorcas had made while she was still with them" (Acts 9:39).

And here's what happened to Tabitha that caused her to be remembered, however briefly, in the New Testament: Peter knelt beside her bed, prayed, and then spoke directly to her saying, "Tabitha, get up" (v. 40). And she did! She arose from the dead!

I'm looking forward to visiting with Tabitha someday. If she was a good and dedicated disciple *before* she was raised from the dead, can you just imagine what she became afterward?

I guess we'll never know, until we meet her in heaven. And won't that be fun, getting to know these "nobodies" and celebrating all the amazing but unrecorded work they did for the Lord? I'm thinking we're gonna need a really big coffeepot for that heavenly kaffeeklatsch!

NOBODIES WHO WERE PART OF GOD'S PLAN

Now let's briefly consider some other nobody women who are briefly mentioned in the Bible because of their impact on their husbands. These two played very minor roles in biblical history—one bad, one good—but their actions were all part of God's plan.

First let's look at Potiphar's lustful and lying wife in the Old Testament story of Joseph, the son of Rachel and Jacob, discussed back in chapter 5. Joseph's jealous brothers sold him into slavery, and in Egypt he was bought by Potiphar, captain of Pharaoh's guard.

Joseph quickly became Potiphar's most trusted servant; in fact Genesis 39:6 says Potiphar "left in Joseph's care everything he had; with Joseph in charge, he did not concern himself with anything except the food he ate."

Joseph was quite handsome, and Potiphar's wife "took notice of Joseph and said, 'Come to bed with me!' . . . And though she spoke to Joseph day after day, he refused to go to bed with her or even be with her" (vv. 7, 12).

One day Potiphar's wife managed to get Joseph's cloak away from him, and later she showed it to her husband and lied to him. saying Joseph "came in here to sleep with me, but I screamed" (v. 14).

Outraged, Potiphar threw Joseph in prison . . . where, once again, he demonstrated goodness and kindness to those around him and quickly won the trust of the warden, who "put Joseph in charge of all those held in the prison, and he was made responsible for all that was done there" (v. 22).

While he was in prison, God gave Joseph the gift of interpreting dreams. When two of Pharaoh's servants, the baker and the cupbearer, fell from favor and landed in prison, Joseph accurately interpreted their disturbing dreams. He told the baker that he would be executed, and he assured the cupbearer he would be restored to Pharaoh's household staff. A couple of years later, when Pharaoh had a disturbing dream, the cupbearer remembered Joseph's gift and told Pharaoh, who summoned Joseph.

You already know the rest of the story, how Joseph interpreted Pharaoh's dream, won his trust, and was put in charge of stockpiling the kingdom's resources in preparation for the famine that would eventually bring Joseph's brothers to Egypt seeking relief. But what can we learn from it, especially the role of Potiphar's wife? Well, here's the big-picture lesson: that woman's treachery landed Joseph in prison despite his innocence, and while he was there he may have asked, "What's goin' on, Lord?" But his heart stayed true to God, and *eventually God's plan was revealed*.

We also learn we wouldn't want to include Mrs. P in our circle of girlfriends; that's for sure! But we also see how God can use someone, maybe an unbeliever, to put us in a tough spot. And while we're in that difficult situation, he is with us; he may be preparing us and possibly gifting us for the next step in his plan.

The next time someone wrongs you, remember Potiphar's wife and how she wronged Joseph—and by doing so put him in exactly the right spot to meet Pharaoh's cupbearer.

Next let's take a quick look at another high-class nobody, Pilate's wife. Matthew 27 tells how the story began: "The chief priests and the elders of the people came to the decision to put Jesus to death. They bound him, led him away and handed him over to Pilate, the governor" (vv. 1–2).

So the questioning began, and in the middle of it Pilate received this urgent message from his wife: "Don't have anything to do with that innocent man, for I have suffered a great deal today in a dream because of him" (v. 19).

We don't know if this was a routine wifely interruption for Pilate or a one-time thing. But we know Pilate tried to heed his wife's advice. John 19:8 says Pilate was afraid, and John 19:12 says, "Pilate tried to set Jesus free." He gave the angry Jews a choice; he named two prisoners and let them pick the one he would release—hoping, no doubt, they would choose to release Jesus. Instead, they loudly chose Barabbas, a bandit, and urged Pilate to crucify Jesus. The next verses in Matthew 27 are a dramatic march toward Calvary:

> "Why? What crime has he committed?" asked Pilate. But they shouted all the louder, "Crucify him!"
>
> When Pilate saw that he was getting nowhere, but that instead an uproar was starting, he took water and washed his hands in front of the crowd. "I am innocent of this man's blood," he said. "It is your responsibility!"
>
> All the people answered, "Let his blood be on us and on our children!"
>
> Then he released Barabbas to them. But he had Jesus flogged, and handed him over to be crucified. (vv. 23–26)

The role of Pilate's wife in the story of Jesus's cruel death and glorious resurrection is nothing more than a side note, a brief interruption, a momentary pause caused by a nobody we never hear from again. The crucifixion went on as Jesus knew it inevitably would. But because we know that nothing is in Scripture by accident, it's intriguing to consider why God gave Pilate's wife the dream that caused her to suffer "a great deal."

Could it be that later, when the earth trembled and the sky darkened unexpectedly, or when the centurion came with news that Jesus's body was gone, Pilate and his wife remembered her dream and changed their lives for the good? We don't know. So we're left to ponder why God sent this nobody this dream and what happened because of it. I'd like to think it eventually caused Pilate's wife to become a believer. But such a hope reminds me that if Pilate's wife didn't become a believer back then, she's definitely a believer now that she's reached eternity!

Her story also teaches us that sometimes all the details of God's plan will remain a mystery to us until we get to heaven (or don't!). We may not know at the time why the events that shape our lives unfold as they do. But we can be assured that God knows.

BEHIND EVERY MAN . . .

Mrs. Noah is also a woman who might be considered a nobody since she's barely mentioned—and never named. We know she lived during a terrible time when people were so wicked God regretted that he had ever created human beings at all (see Genesis 6:5–6). The Noahs lived in a world that was "corrupt in God's sight and full of violence" (v. 11).

She must have had to zip her lips and grind her teeth to keep from mouthing off while her scornful neighbors ridiculed her husband for building something nobody had ever heard of for a reason nobody could believe.

Have you ever lived in a place that was "full of violence"? Sad to say, such places are plentiful today. Imagine trying to keep your family safe in a place where the sounds of gunfire are all too common. Where you have a half-dozen locks on your doors—and thieves still manage to break in. Where filthy language and illegal drugs are an everyday thing. Many wives and mothers are out there today, living in conditions like that. I imagine things were equally bad—or worse—right before the flood.

It was in that environment that Mrs. Noah sent her good husband off to work every day to build what the community surely thought was a fool's dream. There's no tellin' what her neighbors said to her as they all carried water together from the well or hung out clothes to dry or pulled weeds in their gardens: "Well, well, well, Mrs. N. I see your husband's down there working on his *lark* again—er, I mean, *ark*." "Better not hang your clothes out here in the *desert* today, Mrs. Noah. It might *rain* for the first time in a zillion years."

I can see her biting her lip, smiling tightly and nodding, and going on about her business, trying to ignore how others disparaged her hardworking husband and their family.

That's a situation I know just a little about. After all, I grew up during the Jim Crow era. Most of the time I was able to control my temper and "just go on about your business, girl, and don't pay them no never mind," as Granny taught me. Ah, but there was that one time . . .

I started college during the early days of the civil rights movement, when the only dorm room the university's black female students were allowed to occupy was a cubbyhole in the basement next to the boiler room. Five of us lived in that little space.

There were just a handful of African-American students on campus, and while there were plenty of fellow students who were kind to us, or at least ignored us, we also became accustomed to being stared at, whispered about, and commented on. One day my roommate Doris let me step in front of her when she was standing in the lunch line. Immediately another girl in the line yelled, "Did you see what that n—— did?"

Well, before I knew what I was doing, I had jumped on that girl, knocked her down, and was fixing to pummel away on her when my friends managed to pull me off her. Evidently I just plain lost my mind that day. I was sent to the dean's office and might have been kicked out, but I had never gotten in trouble before, and my grades were good, so I was allowed to stay but put on probation for the rest of the year. The other girl was moved out of the dorm.

Probation meant I had to be in my room down in the basement every night by 6 p.m., and I couldn't participate in any extracurricular activities. Now, that wasn't all that bad a punishment, because black students weren't allowed to participate in any of those activities anyway. So it wasn't all that bad. The worst part was hearing that girl's words echoing through my mind over and over again.

I bring this up now to say I can empathize with the disparagement we assume Noah and his family faced while he was building that ark. I know what it's like to be ridiculed and called names. Thank goodness Noah and his family evidently didn't give in to the urge to pounce on some of those naysayers—didn't knock 'em down and beat the tar out of 'em. Who knows what might have happened if they had done that? After all, "Noah was six hundred years old when the floodwaters came on the earth" (Genesis 7:6), so we have to assume Mrs. Noah was no spring chicken either.

And think of the work she faced once she and the rest of her brood were locked up together inside the ark. Although the Bible doesn't mention it, I suspect she took charge of the floating household, planning the meals and doing the laundry. (Have you ever wondered . . . did they eat *meat* during those forty days and nights on the ark? Did Noah bring along some extra chickens and goats?)

Imagine what a job it was to clean up after all those stinky animals and birds and bugs. Of course we hope Noah and his sons did the poop-scoopin' and stall-cleanin', but I'm sure there was plenty of work left for Mrs. Noah and her daughters-in-law to do.

Amazingly, when I study the story of the flood, I don't see any mention of anyone going stir crazy on the ark, and that may be what I admire most about Mrs. Noah. I like to imagine that, like us moms today, she set the tone for the household; I like to think she had a joyful attitude that overcame the frayed tempers, building frustration, and overwhelming stench of those who were bobbing on the waves of the water. In short, I credit her with somehow managing to keep her family members from killing each other while they were cooped up together those long forty days and forty nights.

Again, I can empathize, but in this case I fall far short of the high standard I credit Mrs. Noah for setting in enduring so much family togetherness. In my previous book, *Listen Up, Honey,* I wrote about the frequent family gatherings at our home in Dallas. Girl, when those kids and grandkids and great-grandkids and all the in-laws, outlaws, and hangers-on show up after church, my house is ready to burst at the seams (or whatever it is that holds houses together).

We have a wild time, eatin' and laughin' and talkin' and jokin'. The men watch TV, the women sit around the table solving all the world's problems, and the kids run wild. It's a wonderful day . . . right up until five o'clock or so. Then I'm ready for everyone to leave. Being the gracious hostess I am, I may start dropping subtle clues, yawning and blinking my eyes real big, hoping they'll take the hint. Of course that never works; by that time they're all having fun and not paying any attention to me at all. So maybe I'll start picking up stuff, tidying the kitchen, carrying their coats and purses and dishes to the door.

No one notices.

So finally I announce in my sternest Mama T voice: "I'm tired. Y'all need to go home!"

That never works either.

If I'm lucky, sometime around seven or eight—after we've dragged out the lunch leftovers and had another messy feast—I'll manage to get the last one out the door.

Knowing how exhausted I am after one full day of family fun, I think of Mrs. Noah and admire all over again the love and patience and fortitude she must have had to bring her family through that long ordeal of too much family togetherness without any of them losing their mind or killing anyone!

We can only imagine, as God closed the door of the ark and the floodwaters rose, that all those on the ark realized the awesome power of God's might. How privileged—and loved—they must have felt to have been the only ones spared from the disaster that wiped out all other living creatures. We have to believe that all that family togetherness also brought them closer to their Father God.

Oh, that we could live our lives today remembering in every moment what Mrs. Noah and her family knew on the ark, that our lives are completely, totally, entirely in God's hands! She might have been a nobody, but she knew the truth.

THE OTHER EXTREME: MRS. JOB

Now, I'm making a lot of assumptions about Mrs. Noah. The Bible doesn't actually say whether she was supportive of Noah through their experience or whether he had to drag her into the ark kicking and screaming. But the tone of the story seems to imply that she was a contributing member of the family team, and that's what I choose to believe about her.

On the other hand, we don't have to guess about the reaction of another unnamed wife when calamity befell her spouse. Mrs. Job's husband was "blameless and upright; he feared God and shunned evil. . . He was the greatest man among all the people of the East" (Job 1:1, 3). Mrs. Job, in contrast . . . well, we can learn from her mistake.

God was so proud of Job, he pointed him out to Satan one day, asking, "Have you considered my servant Job?" (v. 8).

Satan's reply, put in modern language in *The Message*, was,

> So do you think Job does all that out of the sheer goodness of his heart? Why, no one ever had it so good! You pamper him like a pet, make sure nothing bad ever happens to him or his family or his possessions, bless everything he does— he can't lose! But what do you think would happen if you reached down and took away everything that is his? He'd curse you right to your face, that's what. (vv. 9–11, MSG)

Poor ol' Job was down there on earth, worshiping God and minding his own business, with no clue about the celestial conversation going on about him or the disasters that were about to befall him.

God assured Satan he could do whatever he wanted to Job, and Job would remain true to his Lord. The only thing

God said Satan couldn't do was kill Job. Everything else was allowed.

So now let's put ourselves in Mrs. Job's sandals. She and her family were kickin' in high cotton. They had servants and cooks, a mansion surrounded by beautiful fields, huge herds of livestock, plenty of money, and surely everything a woman of that time could ever want. I can just picture the color draining from her face as Satan began his evil attack. First Satan took away all Job's livestock and killed his herdsmen and servants. Then he killed all ten of Job's children. Finally he covered Job with boils from the bottoms of his feet to the top of his head.

Understandably, Job's wife was distraught and angry at what was happening to them for no apparent reason. Put yourself in her place, and it's easy to understand why, in overwhelming anguish, she urged Job to "curse God and die!" (Job 2:9).

But Job refused. While he scratched his raw, festering sores with a broken piece of pottery, he answered, "You are talking like a foolish woman. Shall we accept good from God, and not trouble?" (v. 10).

Now, here's what I find extremely interesting about Job and his wife: God allowed Satan to do anything he wanted to Job except kill him, and Satan took away everything

Job owned, killed off all ten of his children, and then afflicted him with boils. But notice that Satan did not take away Job's wife. And given how she reacted to her husband—evidently urging him to kill himself—I have to wonder if her continued existence wasn't part of the trials Satan deliberately unleashed against Job! Oh, dear Jesus! Help me *never* be such a source of discouragement to my husband. As I study the story of Job and his wife, help me learn from *her* . . . and be more like *him*!

Job was steadfast in his devotion to God. Even though his three friends joined his wife in trying to convince him otherwise (no doubt, giving rise to the question, With friends like these, who needs enemies?), Job never stopped believing God loved him. He never stopped trusting that God had a plan for him, and that plan would eventually prove beneficial.

And that's exactly what happened. Satan did everything he could to Job and never managed to dent Job's faith one bit. So he gave up. And what do you know? God restored to Job everything he had taken away . . . and then some. He gave him twice as many animals as he had owned before, and he had Job's brothers, sisters, and friends deliver gifts of money and gold to him (see Job 42:10–12). And even though his wife had been a badmouthing pain in the neck, Job apparently forgave her and loved her still. I say this because, after God restored all that wealth to Job, "God also gave him seven more sons and three more daughters" (v. 13 TLB)!

Partners in Evangelism

We've looked at Mrs. Noah, the silent, supportive wife, and Mrs. Job, the faithless wife who urged her besieged husband to "curse God and die." Now let's take a quick look at another "nobody" wife who's rarely remembered when we talk about heroes of the faith. Unlike Mrs. Noah, who stayed in the background, or Mrs. Job, who would have pulled her husband away from God, Priscilla, wife of Aquila, joined her husband in loving the Lord and worked side by side with him to spread the gospel. Everywhere Aquila is mentioned in the New Testament, Priscilla is mentioned also. And most of the time, she's named first!

They were living in Corinth as exiles from Rome (after Emperor Claudius commanded all Jews to leave), when the apostle Paul arrived there. Acts 18:3 says, "Because he was a tentmaker as they were, he stayed and worked with them." Paul also preached in the synagogue, and it seems obvious that he shared the gospel with Priscilla and Aquila, because, after spending a year and a half in Corinth, Paul moved on to Ephesus, and Priscilla and Aquila went with him.

Since the husband and wife are always mentioned together, we have to believe they were equal partners in their evangelistic work. Acts 18 tells us Paul left the couple in Ephesus, where they evidently worked on their own to spread the gospel. They didn't seem to raise a ruckus and shout out the good news from street corners. They weren't big-name evangelists whose wisdom is quoted in beloved Scripture passages today. But they were devoted to the Lord. Paul called them "my fellow workers in Christ Jesus" (Romans 16:3).

Most impressively, during this time soon after the crucifixion, when Christians were often condemned, outcast, and even attacked by unbelievers, Priscilla and Aquila bravely opened their home to Christian gatherings. In fact, twice Paul made reference to "the church that is in their house" (Romans 16:5, 1 Corinthians 16:19 NKJV).

From what little we know of them, Priscilla and her husband seemed to have been quiet and gracious people. We see this in the gentle way they corrected another Christian evangelist who came to Ephesus. Apollos was "a terrific speaker, eloquent and powerful in his preaching of the Scriptures. He was well-educated in the way of the

Master and fiery in his enthusiasm" (Acts 18:24–25 MSG).

But when Priscilla and Aquila heard him speak, they realized he hadn't heard "the rest of the story." He knew about the baptism of John, but he didn't know about the crucifixion and resurrection! Now, Priscilla and Aquila could have corrected him in public as he was preaching. Or they could have scoffed at his ignorance, questioning how he could be in the field of evangelism and not know about this most astounding event.

Instead they "took him aside and told him the rest of the story" (v. 26 MSG). As a result of their kind encouragement, Apollos went on to other cities where he was "a great help to those who by grace had believed" (v. 27). And "he vigorously refuted the Jews in public debate, proving from the Scriptures that Jesus was the Christ" (v. 28).

Maybe Priscilla and Aquila recognized Apollos's gift for public speaking and preaching; maybe it was a gift they didn't possess themselves. So they worked with him to improve his message, then they sent him on his way to reach out to those they couldn't reach themselves.

When I read about Priscilla and her husband—when I consider what they knew and what I can learn from them—I see courage, humility, and devotion to each other and to the gospel.

BECOMING A WOMAN
OTHERS CAN LEARN FROM

We can't all be "terrific speaker[s], eloquent, and powerful." But we can support someone who may be serving the Lord in a way we can't. Perhaps we can open our homes to a Christian women's group or a Bible study. Maybe we can even start a ministry. (Look at me—I was a nobody, and I've started two!) Or maybe we can just take some girlfriends aside—invite them out for coffee or lunch—and find an opening for introducing them to the gospel.

I remember reading a line somewhere that reminded us we don't have to do grand and impressive things ourselves to change the world. By simply living our lives in a Christlike way, we may inspire grand and wonderful things in others. As a result, that other writer said, "You may be the one who touches the one who changes the world."

In this book I've described women who've done both. Some did grand and impressive things—like Esther, who risked death to speak up for her people. Others, like Rhoda, simply opened doors (or *meant* to open doors but got so excited they forgot to do it) and/or opened their hearts . . . and God noticed. Doing God's work can begin with the smallest gesture. Jesus said, "Anyone by just giving you a cup of water in my name is on our side. Count on it that God will notice" (Mark 9:41 MSG).

Sometimes, simply by sharing how faith worked in our lives, we may inspire others to hang on for one more day when the darkness seems to be closing in. Maybe we can light one little spark in them that will eventually kindle a fire of passion for God. I want to close this book with another story from my life that I hope will do that for you.

Because my husband and I are in business for ourselves, insurance has been an expensive problem for us. When the monthly premiums became too much of a financial burden for us, we decided we would drop our insurance coverage and do our best to become self-insured. We dutifully saved money every month in a health fund, and when I had to have that hysterectomy, we paid those bills in cash. No problem.

Then came the complications and the emergency second surgery, the days in ICU, and all that other stuff. When the bill came for all those procedures, it was more than $26,000, and our health fund had been depleted. I prayed day and night, asking God what I should do, how I would pay that bill.

One morning I looked at that bill and thought, *This is*

not right. Well, it might have been right in the hospital's eyes, but through *my* eyes it was terribly inflated. So I called the hospital's billing office and said, "I'm calling to tell you I'm not paying this bill."

"What?"

"Let me tell you why I'm not paying it," I said. "This bill is inflated. When you take all the inflation out of the bill and send me my real bill, I'll pay it."

Well, in three days they sent me an "adjusted" bill . . . for $11,900.

Now, girl, a lot of people get nervous when I start talking about how God works to handle specific problems in my life, especially money problems. Many Christians have a completely different relationship with God than I do. They trust God as I do, but they don't expect the miracles I've experienced again and again. And I know full well that sometimes God says no. Sometimes Thelma Wells has to fall on her face and work her way back up. When that happens, I know it's God's will and he's intending for me to learn something out of that difficult experience. But what I'm telling you now is how God handled this problem—and I hope it will inspire you to let him handle your problems too.

I said, "OK, God, thank you for prodding the hospital to send me this smaller bill. Thank you, God! I praise you,

God! But, you know, I don't have $11,900 either. And, dear Jesus, you knew before the foundation of the world that I was going to have *two* surgeries, and you knew I was going to need the money to pay both bills. So I thank you for whatever you're gonna do to get me through this situation. And, just as a reminder, Lord, the bill's due in a couple of weeks—January 21."

Three days later I got a letter from a financial firm about an investment I'd forgotten I had. Something had matured, and what did I want them to do with it?

Guess how much the investment was: 11,900-some dollars.

I called the financial company and said, "I need to cash this thing out. Can I do it without penalty?"

They said, "You could have cashed it out when you were fifty-nine and a half." (I won't go into detail about how long ago that was.) They told me the procedure for cashing out the investment, and in a couple of days, the check came, we deposited it, and I wrote a check to the hospital for the complete balance on January 20.

I believe every promise God has given me. I stand on every promise he's made, especially the promise that he will "supply all your needs according to His riches in glory in Christ Jesus" (Philippians 4:19 NASB).

When you look back at the stories of the women in this book, see the rewards that came to those who knew and trusted God. See the calamities that befell those who didn't. Learn from what they knew. Learn from what they learned the hard way.

And pass on the gift.

We'd love to hear from you about your experience with this book. Please go to **www.thomasnelson.com/letusknow** for a quick and easy way to give us your feedback.

Love to read? Get excerpts from new books sent to you by email. Join Shelf Life, Thomas Nelson's FREE online book club. Go to **www.thomasnelson.com/shelflife**.